TEXT/URES OF IRAQ
CONTEMPORARY ART FROM
THE COLLECTION OF ODED HALAHMY

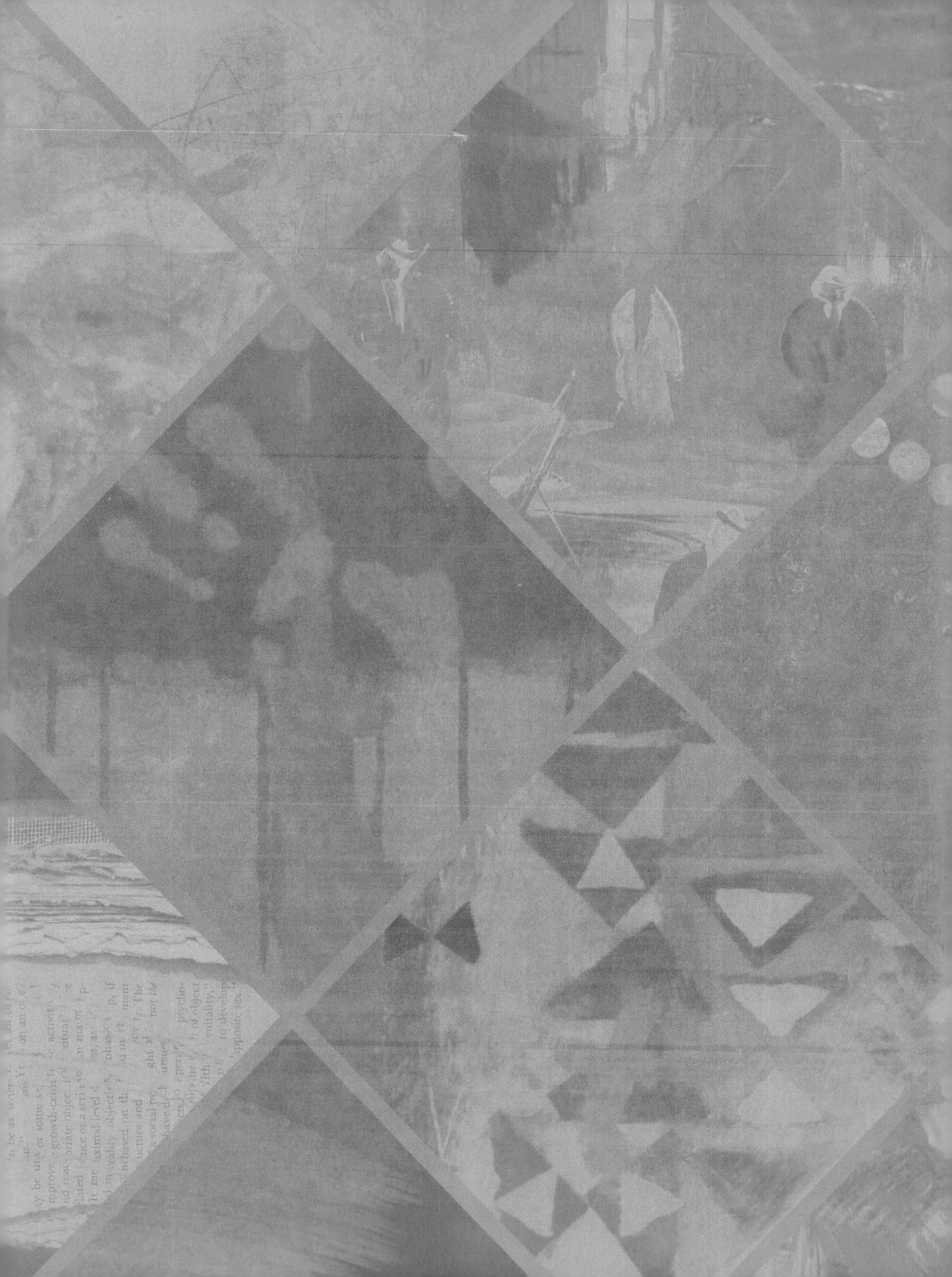

TEXT/URES OF IRAQ

CONTEMPORARY ART FROM
THE COLLECTION OF ODED HALAHMY

CURATED BY
MURTAZA VALI

WITH CONTRIBUTIONS BY
ODED HALAHMY
SARA J. PASTI

SAMUEL DORSKY MUSEUM OF ART
STATE UNIVERSITY OF
NEW YORK AT NEW PALTZ

Published on the occasion of the exhibition *Text/ures of Iraq: Contemporary Art from the Collection of Oded Halahmy*, curated by Murtaza Vali, on display from February 4 – May 21, 2017 in the Howard Greenberg Family Gallery of the Samuel Dorsky Museum of Art, State University of New York at New Paltz.

Support for The Dorsky Museum's exhibitions and programs is provided by the Friends of the Samuel Dorsky Museum of Art and the State University of New York at New Paltz. Additional support for the exhibition and catalogue has been provided by the Dorsky Museum Contemporary Art Program Fund.

Published by the Samuel Dorsky Museum of Art
State University of New York at New Paltz
One Hawk Drive
New Paltz, New York 12561

Designed by Jeffrey Peltzman
Edited by Ursula Morgan, Coordinator of Exhibitions and Programs,
Samuel Dorsky Museum of Art, State University of New York at New Paltz
Translation by Amera Abdalhafez
Printed by Lightning Source
Distributed by the State University of New York Press
(www.sunypress.edu)

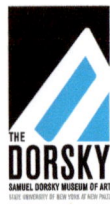
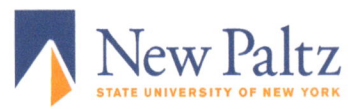

CONTENTS

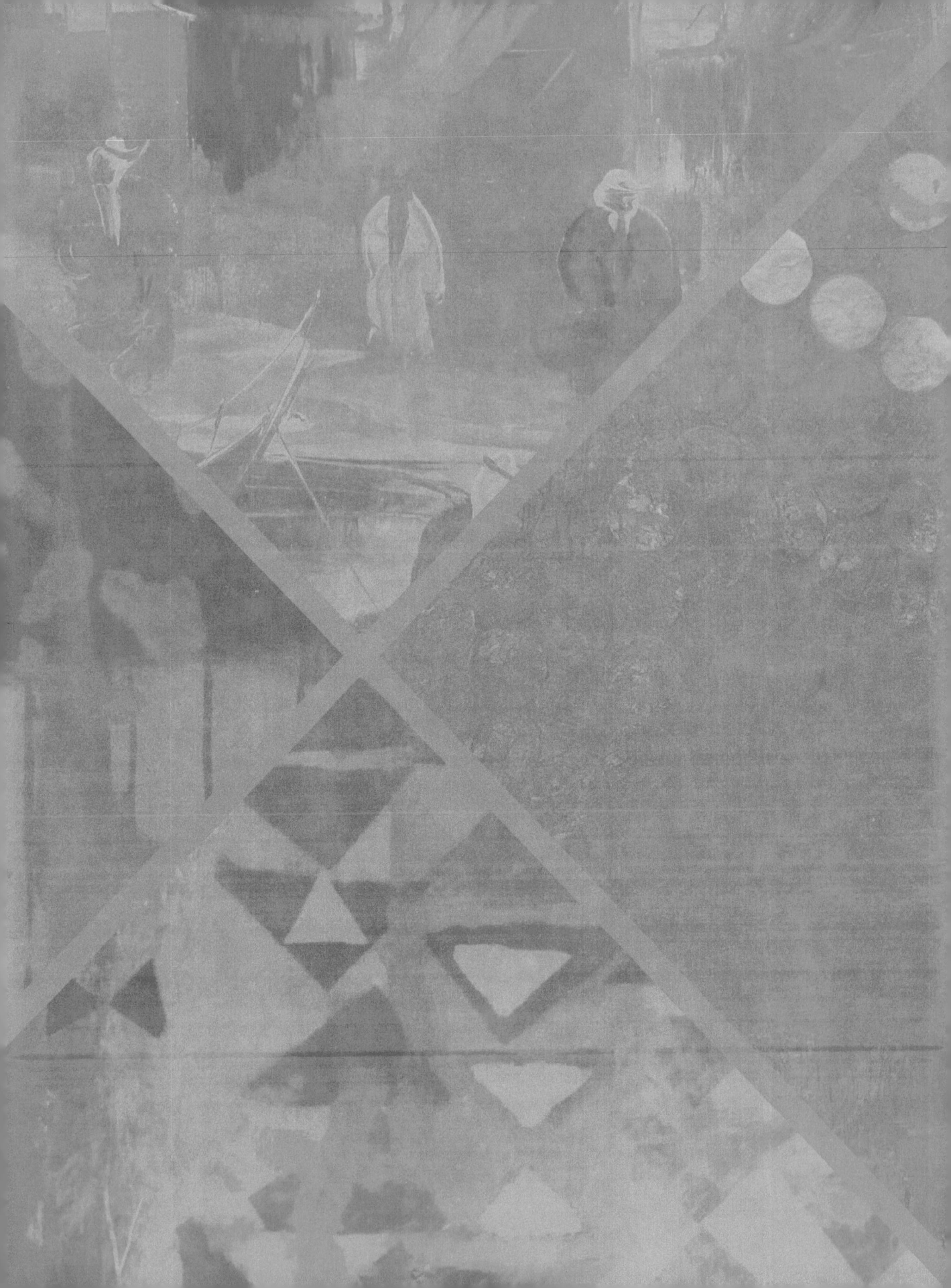

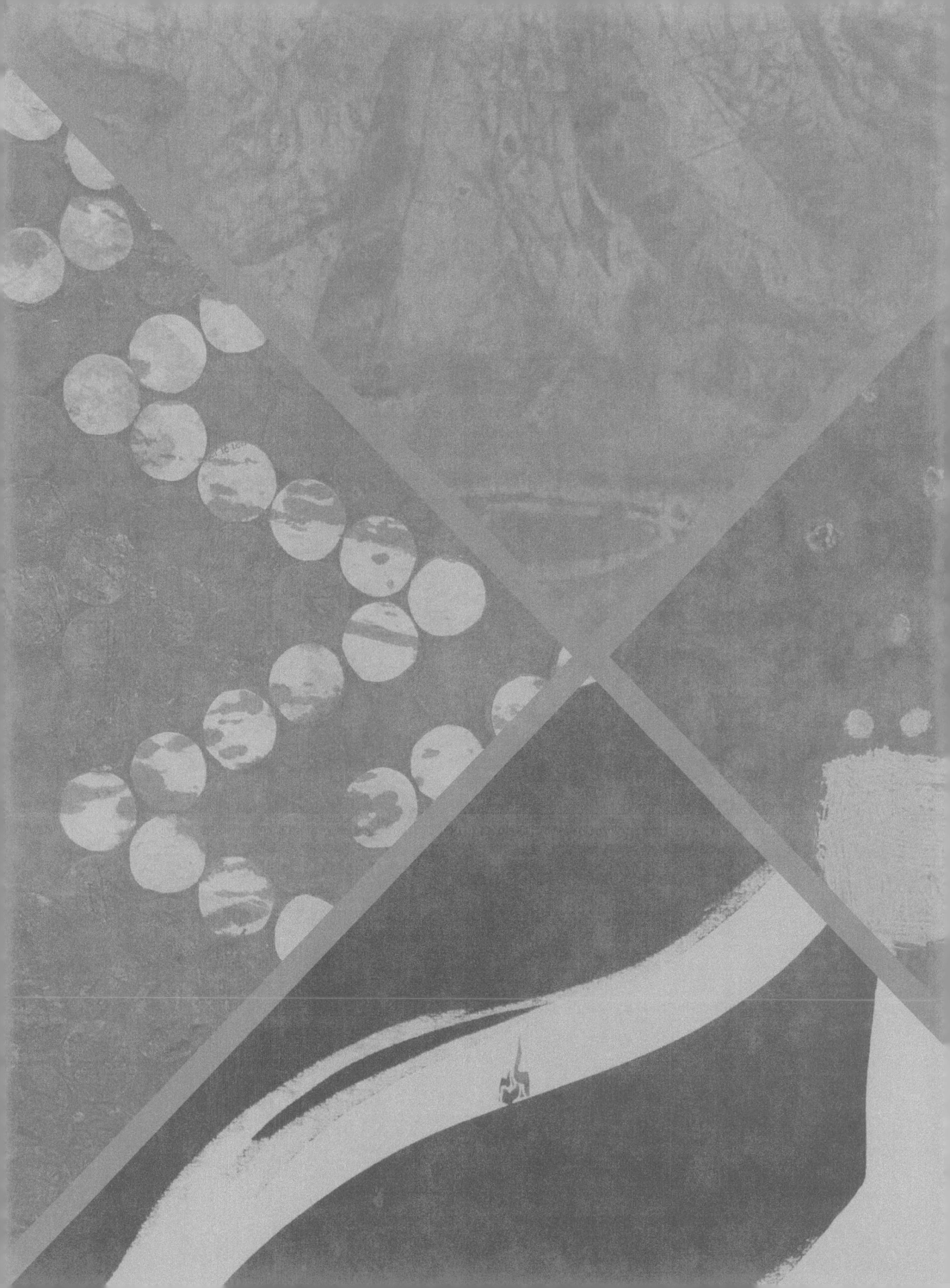

FOREWORD

SARA J. PASTI
THE NEIL C. TRAGER DIRECTOR
SAMUEL DORSKY MUSEUM OF ART

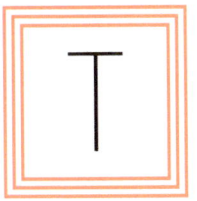The mission of the Samuel Dorsky Museum of Art is to support and enrich the academic programs at the university and to present a broad range of national and international art for public education, study, and enjoyment. Underlying this language is an understanding that the goal of presenting national and international art is to enhance understanding of the diverse cultures that exist in the region, the country, and the world.

A native of Baghdad, Iraq, artist and collector Oded Halahmy emigrated to Israel in 1951. His primary interests include supporting Iraqi artists and promoting international understanding through art and artist exchanges. In 2002, to encourage peace in the Middle East, Halahmy founded The Oded Halahmy Foundation for the Arts, Inc., a non-profit cultural organization created to fund original artistic expression of peace and hope in the Middle East. In 2006, Halahmy opened the Pomegranate Gallery, a New York City–based gallery dedicated to exhibiting contemporary Middle Eastern artists.

Text/ures of Iraq: Contemporary Art from the Collection of Oded Halahmy is a unique presentation for the museum because it brings to our campus art from a part of the world—the Middle East—that is relatively unknown to most people living in this country. The work shown here is rough and sophisticated, wonderfully colorful and somber, and, above all, amazingly soulful, deriving from the artists' imaginations, from art history, and from lives lived in a war zone.

Through the art presented in the exhibition, through this publication, and through a wide range of public programs, museum visitors will enrich their understanding of contemporary Iraqi art practice as well as the ideas and themes of an age-old tradition that have inspired artists for many centuries. We hope that audiences will find something to inspire them in this exhibition, just as the artists in this exhibition have themselves been inspired.

I am grateful to Oded Halahmy for the generous loan of his collection and his support and participation in the exhibition and its accompanying programs. I am also grateful to David Dorsky, who first introduced me to Oded Halahmy. Additional thanks go to catalogue designer Jeffrey Peltzman, who worked with Ursula Morgan, The Dorsky's Interim Coordinator of Exhibitions and Programs, to develop this publication. Last but not least, I extend my personal gratitude to the members of The Dorsky's Advisory Board and Program Committee, and to Dorsky Museum staff members Janis Benincasa, Zachary Bowman, Wayne Lempka, Amy Pickering, and Bob Wagner, without whom the museum's exhibitions and programs would not be possible.

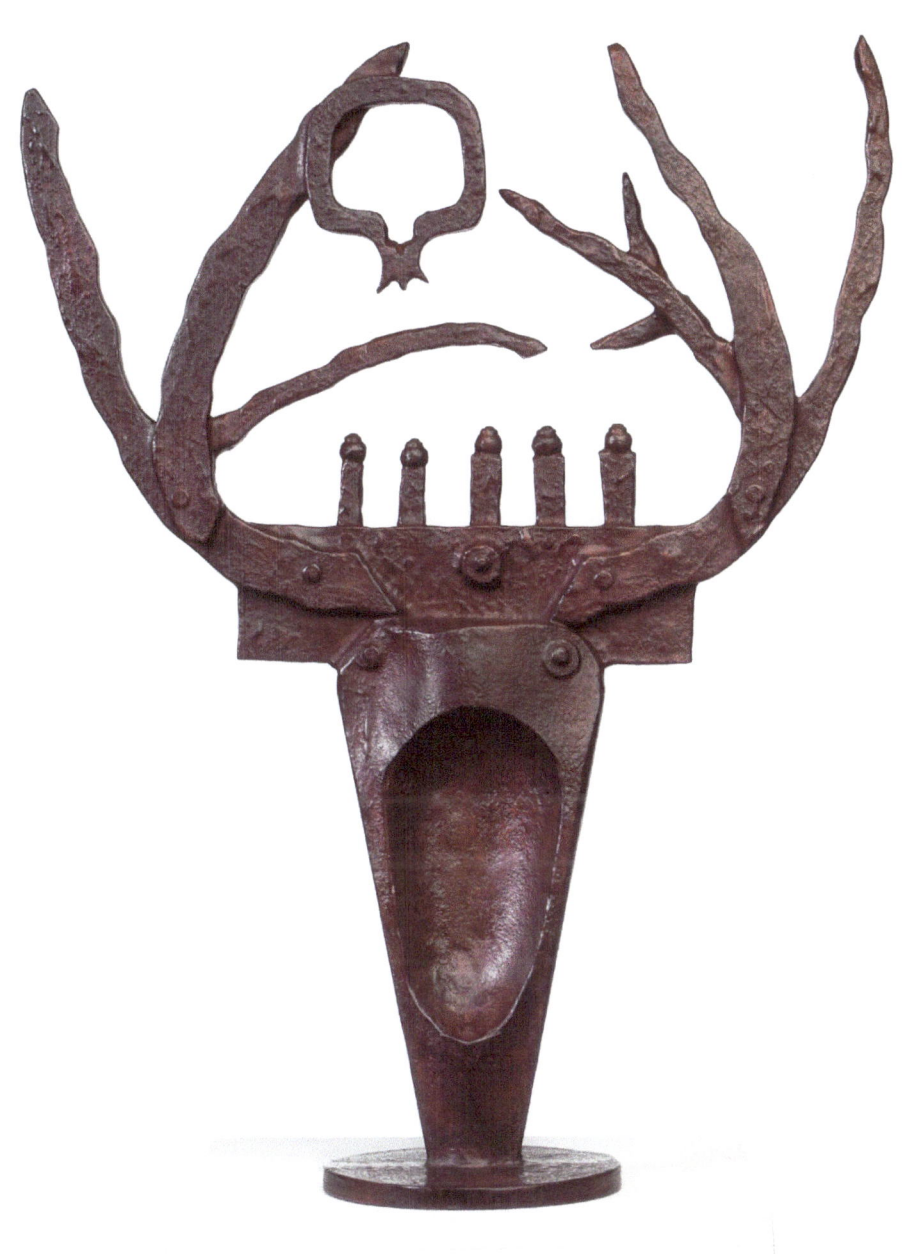

Oded Halahmy, *Babylon is My Home*, 2006, bronze cast, 28¾ x 22½ x 7¾ in.

COLLECTOR'S STATEMENT

ODED HALAHMY

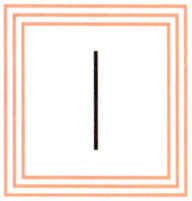 always felt that I could do more to support and promote Iraqi art and culture. Because of this I established the Oded Halahmy Foundation for the Arts. I wanted Westerners to be aware that beyond oil, the Middle East has a beautiful culture full of art, poetry, music, and food. To introduce this culture to the United States, I invited Iraqi poets, writers, and musicians from all ethnic backgrounds to read, perform, and exhibit at the Pomegranate Gallery. Through this foundation, I have supported Iraqi artists and promoted Iraqi books that were originally written in Arabic or Hebrew and then translated to English for the American public. I intend to continue doing this work as long as I am able.

The opportunity to exhibit my art with other Iraqi artists finally came about with the 2002 exhibition *Strokes of Genius* at Grinnell College in Iowa. It was a wonderful feeling to be a part of it, and I felt at home among the other artists.

In March 2003, when the United States' war with Iraq began, I felt sad and found it impossible to create and concentrate on my art. In all my years, my love for my Iraqi homeland has never changed and for as long as I can remember since leaving, I had dreamed of visiting Iraq again. It was then a great surprise when my foundation was invited to Iraq to document the status of the Iraqi Jewish holy sites and to encourage their restoration, with the intention of promoting tourism in post–war Iraq. The Foundation was the only organization invited by the Iraqi Cultural Ministry to help with this vision. Known as the El Awakaf, it is responsible for the Muslim, Christian, and Jewish holy sites throughout the country.

The thought of returning to my homeland with the possibility that I could help to preserve Iraq's immense cultural heritage was exciting to me. Until that point in my life I had only been able to visit Iraq in my dreams and through my artwork. However, in 2004 after decades of longing, I landed at Baghdad International Airport. No words can describe the happiness I felt when I stepped out of that plane. I felt that I was finally home.

"Salaam aliekum, ana Iraqi" (Hello, I'm an Iraqi), were my first words to the border policewoman. "Ahlan wa sahlan" (You are welcome), she replied while she stamped my passport. As an Iraqi Jew who travels frequently to Middle East countries, I expect to be questioned at airports. For the first time, however, I was amazed to be welcomed simply with a smile.

My trip coincided with a sudden deterioration of the security situation and the scope of my trip's mission became limited. However, while there I had the privilege of gaining access to the museums, which the American Army did not have the foresight to secure. Though some of the ancient Iraqi artifacts remained unscathed, much of museum's collections were heavily damaged or lost to looters.

With all of the destruction in Iraq, I was still looking for the beautiful things I remembered—I always feel like "my cup is half full." I walked along the rivers, saw the tall palm trees dancing in the wind, visited the coffee and teahouses, viewed the antiquities at the shuttered museums, and visited the old synagogue. I even walked along Al-Mutanabbi Street, the famous market for books where I used to go with my father and mother to buy textbooks for school.

A second visit to my homeland occurred in 2008, when I was able to visit the Yazidi and Kurdish people in the North region and discover their beautiful art, crafts, and culture. On these two visits I had the opportunity to see great contemporary artwork as well as the ancient Babylonian artifacts. Though I was not allowed to carry artwork with me back to the U.S., it remained with me spiritually and energized me to continue supporting Iraqi artists.

I opened the Pomegranate Gallery in SoHo, New York, in 2006 to exhibit Iraqi artists and to serve as a showcase for my Foundation. The first exhibition of Iraqi art presented at the Gallery was titled *Ashes to Art: The Iraqi Phoenix*. Curated by Peter Hastings Falk, the exhibition was attended by the Iraqi Ambassador to the U.S., Samir Shakir Sumaida'ie, among other dignitaries. It was well received by the press and the public who were curious to see what art from Iraq looked like. Later, Navy officer Christopher Brownfield, who had met with each artist in Iraq and brought the exhibition to the United States, organized another exhibition which sold out, with the proceeds benefitting the Iraqi artists. It is wonderful to be able to give back to and interact with artists who still live in Iraq and who have continued to spend their lives creating art in spite of the oppression and chaos that exists there.

Traditionally, Jews and Muslims are not allowed to make imagery that competes with the creation of God. This is one of the objectives of ISIS in Iraq—to destroy any and all religious iconography (such as the Temple at Nimrod). But through my gallery and Foundation, I am dedicated to serving as a cultural bridge and supporter of an ongoing Middle-Eastern peace dialogue, and to creating a space where Iraqi artists of all religious and ethnic backgrounds can exhibit their work in peace and harmony.

I am grateful to David Dorsky who had the foresight to discover my art and that of the Iraqi artists in this exhibition, to his wife Helaine Posner, to Sara Pasti, Director of The Dorsky Museum, and to the President of SUNY New Paltz, Donald Christian, whom I had the pleasure of welcoming to my SoHo studio to see my sculptures and my collection of Iraqi art.

When peace comes in Iraq, we will drink pomegranate cocktails and give a pomegranate to all the Iraqi people around the world.

TEXT/URES OF IRAQ: CONTEMPORARY ART FROM THE COLLECTION OF ODED HALAHMY

MURTAZA VALI

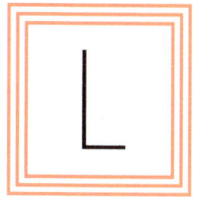iterary culture—letters, words, and books—has been a mainstay of Iraqi culture for many millennia. The ancient civilizations that inhabited the territory constituting modern day Iraq were responsible for the development of cuneiform, one of the earliest systems of writing, and ancient texts like the *Epic of Gilgamesh* and the Code of Hammurabi. In the centuries following the advent of Islam, Baghdad was the most important center of knowledge and learning, home to the *dar al hikma* or House of Wisdom, the largest and most famous library in the world at the time of its destruction in the thirteenth century by invading Mongol armies. In more recent times this literary ethos may be best exemplified by the famous Al-Mutanabbi Street, an old Baghdad thoroughfare jam packed with bookstores and outdoor stalls that has tragically been the target of terror that has plagued the capital and the rest of the country since the turn of the millennium.[1] As the old Arab adage goes, "Cairo Writes, Beirut Publishes, and Baghdad Reads," and despite the decades of war, conflict, and sanctions, the importance given to text in Iraqi society, culture, and visual arts remains.

Text and texture share an etymological root: *texere* or Latin for to weave. This exhibition, drawn from the personal collection of New York–based sculptor Oded Halahmy, a Jewish native of Baghdad, weaves his work in with that of eight contemporary artists from Iraq, using this shared etymology to enmesh the idea of text with that of texture, a quality that can be both resolutely material and elusively affective. While the layered and abraded surfaces of some works index the region's ancient past and/or its violent present, the picturesqueness of others captures the powerful affective textures of nostalgia and exile. Celebrating their country as a pastoral idyll, where people of different beliefs, cultures, and ethnicities peacefully coexisted for centuries, these works also mourn the eventual fraying of the once rich fabric of Iraqi culture.

A modern master, Hassan Massoudy illustrates short phrases and aphorisms extracted from masterworks of both the Arab and Western intellectual traditions, playing with color, scale, and gesture to update the tenets of Arabic calligraphy. *Sur terre, il y a place pour tous, Schiller* (2006) [**Plate 22**], presents a famous line from the German poet and philosopher's *Der Alpenjäger*. Massoudy isolates the Arabic word for "earth," using it as a formal compositional element. Executed in broad brushy blue strokes that resemble Chinese calligraphy, its first three letters are transformed into an S-shaped zigzag that dominates the frame. The whole phrase is written out in black, in a more traditional script, underneath. *The love that I hold for you, that is my eternal delight/The passion that I swear to you, this is my religion, Ibn Zaydoun 11th century* (2008) [**Plate 23**], illustrates a couplet by the famous Andalusian poet. The line equates love and worship and Massoudy repeats its dyadic structure as a pair of wide red strokes.

Despite his innovations, Massoudy's practice is still widely perceived as an extension of traditional calligraphy. In contrast, *hurufiyah*, an influential modern Arab variant of Letterism, enacted a radical rupture from the Islamic past, using Arabic letters as visual signs and painterly gestures rather than as vehicles of linguistic meaning. In such works, Arabic script is understood not as a symbol of the past but as an extension of the present, its appearance firmly embedded in the mundane of the everyday. Indebted to one of its foremost theorists, the Iraqi modernist Shakir Hassan Al Said, Hayder Ali's works in oil on wood and in mixed media on paper fall firmly within the *hurufiyah* tradition.[2] Reduced to illegible scrawls, letters and words reappear on Ali's patchy textured surfaces, resembling graffiti-covered city walls. In the aptly titled *Black Talk* (2005) [**Plate 2**], letters congeal into an ominous black morass in the lower right corner. The upper third of *Untitled* (2004) [**Plate 1**] is filled with bullet hole–like punctures, some plugged up with rolled paper, a more overt reference to the daily experience of war. *America* (2005) [**Plate 3**] features a decorative array of orange, green and white triangles, possibly a playful reference to cuneiform's wedge-shaped marks, another instance of linguistic markers reduced to pure form.

Like many Iraqi artists, Hanaa Malallah draws inspiration from the extraordinary cultural achievements of the many pre-Islamic civilizations that emerged from the territories that constitute modern day Iraq. In *Uruk Wall* (2006) [**Plate 21**],

Malallah attaches little wooden disks, some painted black and white, to a weathered wooden panel to recreate the famous stone cone mosaic pattern that adorns the monumental mud-brick walls and buildings of the titular ancient city. A hallmark of Malallah's practice, the distressed materials and abraded surfaces mimic the materiality of an excavated archaeological site, recreating the ruin and decay resulting from the passage of time. But these same material effects also index the textures and traumas of everyday life through decades of oppression, war, and sanctions. Identical in size, *Uruk Old Love* (2006) [**Plate 20**] features a roughly carved relief pattern of triangles within a carefully incised grid. Much of the pattern, barring two irregular patches which have been sanded away to reveal the lighter grain underneath, is stained a deep almost blood red, suggesting a surface bearing the traces of a deadly massacre or bombing.

Many of Iraq's storied cultural and educational institutions were looted and/ or destroyed during the 2003 U.S.-led invasion, and in the aftermath ruined libraries and the lost books they held emerged as sites of loss and mourning for Iraqi artists and writers.[3] In Qasim Sabti's collages [**Plates 28–31**] the material remains of destroyed books are presented simply, almost clinically, as if subject to careful forensic examination.[4] Splayed and flattened, each cloth bound hardcover is presented vertically. Subtle variations in color and texture across the distressed covers often result in a neat stack of rectangles that recall color field painting. However, the hollowed out spines and the torn shreds of pages that remain attached are powerful reminders of the historical events that led to their destruction. Brutally emptied of the knowledge they once held within, each empty shell serves as a surrogate for a person, each a portrait of and a modest memorial to a life tragically lost. Yet Sabti's careful and tender attention and most minimal of interventions—occasionally an L-shaped cut is made in the cloth which is then pushed aside to reveal the cardboard underneath— resurrects these remains. As art they testify to the resilience of intellectual and cultural life in Baghdad despite its repeated destruction.[5]

In a similar vein, Ismail Khayat's "Anfal Memory" series [**Plates 14-19**] commemorates the countless victims of the genocidal massacre of Kurds and other minorities in the North by Saddam Hussein's regime during the final stages of the war between Iran and Iraq. Throughout this series, and across his broader practice, Khayat repeats the trope of the face/mask. Each iteration is unique, the features contorted into a distinct and grotesque expression of horror and pain. Microscopic scribbles and tiny notations cover the surfaces of the bruised and battered visages. Some are in a mournful grisaille while others are unexpectedly colorful. Oscillating uncertainly between face and mask, they force a face-to-face encounter with the victims of this atrocity, imploring us to acknowledge their testimony as they bear witness to unimaginable suffering, while protecting their humanity behind veneers of studied anguish.

Mohammed al Hamadany's monumental twenty-five painting series "Laylat an Nar (Night of Fire)" (n.d.), provides a rare Iraqi perspective on the 2003 U.S.-led coalition's invasion of Iraq and the devastation wrought through its Shock and Awe tactics. Executed in a brooding muddy palette, a claustrophobic murk permeates the two panels [**Plates 12, 13**] included in this exhibition. While the colors of the Iraqi flag fill the top half of one panel, its vibrant red is sullied by two oily black handprints and one of its green stars is blotted out by brown paint. Intimations of violence abound: paint drips like blood, floating dashed lines suggest both borders and sutures, the latter echoing actual stitches that barely hold close a slit running down the center of a pale floating form that resembles a disembodied bone or limb in the panel's lower half. A spectral form, possibly the imprint of a body, fills the other panel, and is embellished with childlike line drawings in bright red and blue paint. A pervading gloom holds the discreet iconographical and symbolic references together, implicating everyone equally by enveloping all in the fog of war.

Celebrating their country as a pre-modern pastoral idyll, picturesque works by Amal Alwan and Naziha Rashid provide some respite, revealing instead the powerful affective textures of nostalgia. Alwan's *Blue Domed Mosque* (n.d.) [**Plate 7**] presents a scene of daily life in an unnamed village or town, anchored by the titular architectural feature. Commonly found across Iraq, this structure reappears in *Basrah* (n.d.) [**Plate 6**], an important port in the South, nestled in behind a couple of boats. These works bear an unexpected relationship to calligraphy; the figures are often reduced to two or more sweeping brushstrokes, their curves resembling those of Massoudy's modern calligraphy. Rashid, instead, employs more of a folk art idiom in *Woman in the Village* (1999) [**Plate 24**], reducing a comparable scene of rural daily life into a stylized composition of simple shapes and repeated patterns, forgoing the illusion of depth for the flat frontal quality of an icon. In *Nostalgic* (2000) [**Plate 25**], Rashid personifies the titular sentiment as a young Iraqi maiden, a red flower tucked delicately above her left ear, staring at us wistfully. Some of the surfaces in this work—the girl's right arm, the flowerpot, the bird's perch—are broken down into passages of color, form and texture, where these qualities are used intuitively to convey a mood rather than describe a scene.. Forgoing representation altogether, Rashid's *Evil Eye* (2003) [**Plate 26**], and *In the Market* (2006) [**Plate 27**], though small in scale, represent the full potential of this strategy, abstracting their titular experiences, distilling sentiment from the sentimental.

Many of these distinct threads come together in Oded Halahmy's recent cast bronze sculptures. Inspired by recollections of his Baghdad childhood, Halahmy often combines letters and phrases—in Hebrew, Arabic, and English—with other symbols to form talisman-like totems. *Five Six Singing* (Study) (2013) [**Plate 9**] recaptures a fond memory of learning Hebrew through the repeated recitation of an alphabet song—"wow," the sixth letter in the Hebrew alphabet, sits atop "hey," the fifth one, which rests on top of a flat rhombus with the *chamsa* or palm cut out of it. Erupting out of a pomegranate, each component of this stack of signs holds a wealth of personal, cultural, and mystical meaning. In *Sing Hey Wow* (2013) [**Plate 10**], the letters are phonetically spelled out in English, allowing those unfamiliar with Hebrew to join in. This conviviality is echoed by the smiley pomegranate etched into the triangular base, which is cast from the trunk end of an Iraqi date palm frond. Teeming with symbols—linguistic, imagistic, and material—Halahmy's sculptures seem almost apotropaic, protecting against the dull gnawing ache of exile, of separation, both spatial and temporal, and the amnesia that results from it. In each of these works the weight and durability of the cast bronze monumentalizes its subject, making the past permanent, capturing for eternity, the text/ures of Iraq.

Notes

1. On March 5, 2007, a car bomb exploded in Al-Mutanabbi Street destroying much of the neighborhood, leaving it unusable for over a year. To get some sense of the importance Al-Mutanabbi Street holds for Iraqis and non-Iraqis alike see Beau Beausoleil's art and writing project "Al-Mutanabbi Street Starts Here," initiated shortly after the bombing. Writing that emerged from the project has been anthologized in Beau Beausoleil and Deema Shehabi (eds.), *Al-Mutanabbi Street Starts Here: Poets and Writers Respond to the March 5th, 2007, Bombing of Baghdad's "Street of the Booksellers"* (Oakland: PM Press, 2012).

2. For an extended discussion of *hurufiyah* see Charbel Dagher, *Arabic Hurufiyya: Art and Identity*, trans. Samir Mahmoud (Milan: Skira Editore, 2016) and Nada Shabout, *Modern Arab Art: Formation of Arab Aesthetics* (Gainesville, FL: University of Florida Press, 2007).

3. The artist's book, or *dafatir*, has been a particularly vital format for modern and contemporary artists in/from Iraq. See Nada Shabout (ed.), *Dafatir: Contemporary Iraqi Book Art* (Denton, TX: University of North Texas Press, 2007).

4. Sabti's collages were literally borne of one such traumatic event, the April 2003 fire that destroyed the University of Baghdad's College of Fine Arts Library, an institution that held more than seventy thousand titles and was an invaluable resource for generations of artists educated there. In the aftermath, Sabti found many emptied hardcovers at the site and decided to reuse them in collages as a way to symbolically resurrect the lost books and the knowledge they held. See Sylvia Westall, "Artist's work rises from Baghdad's ashes," *REUTERS.com*, July 13, 2012, accessed November 25, 2016. http://reuters.com/article/us-iraq-art-idUSBRE86C0L520120713.

5. While the building of the College of Fine Arts Library has been reconstructed, the collection is yet to be rebuilt. Wafaa Bilal's *168:01* (2016), presented at the Art Gallery of Windsor, Ontario between January 30—April 10, 2016, is a recent artistic attempt to restock the shelves. The project consists of an installation featuring a seventy-two foot long bookshelf holding one thousand blank books, and a Kickstarter campaign through which copies of the blank books may be purchased for twenty-five dollars each. Bilal will replace each purchased book with a real one, and the collection will be shipped to Baghdad once the project ends. See Marta Bausells, "Artist's 'blank books' project seeks to restock historic Baghdad library," *TheGuardian.com*, January 26, 2016, accessed November 25, 2016. https://theguardian.com/artanddesign/2016/jan/26/wafaa-bilal-168-01-blank-books-project-ontario-baghdad-library.

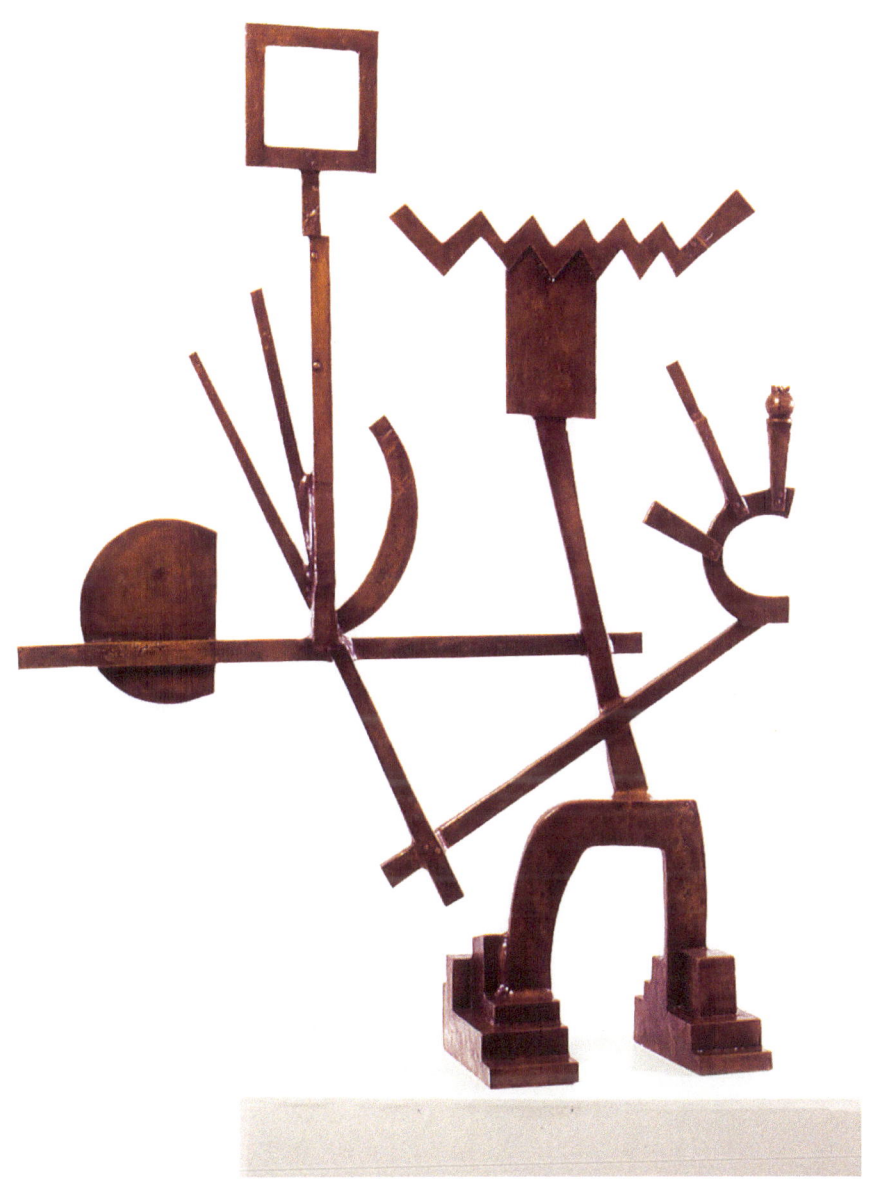

Oded Halahmy, *Royal Figure*, 1985, bronze cast, 52 x 43 x 10 in.

PLATES

Plate 1
Hayder Ali
Untitled, 2004
Oil on wood
24 x 24 in.

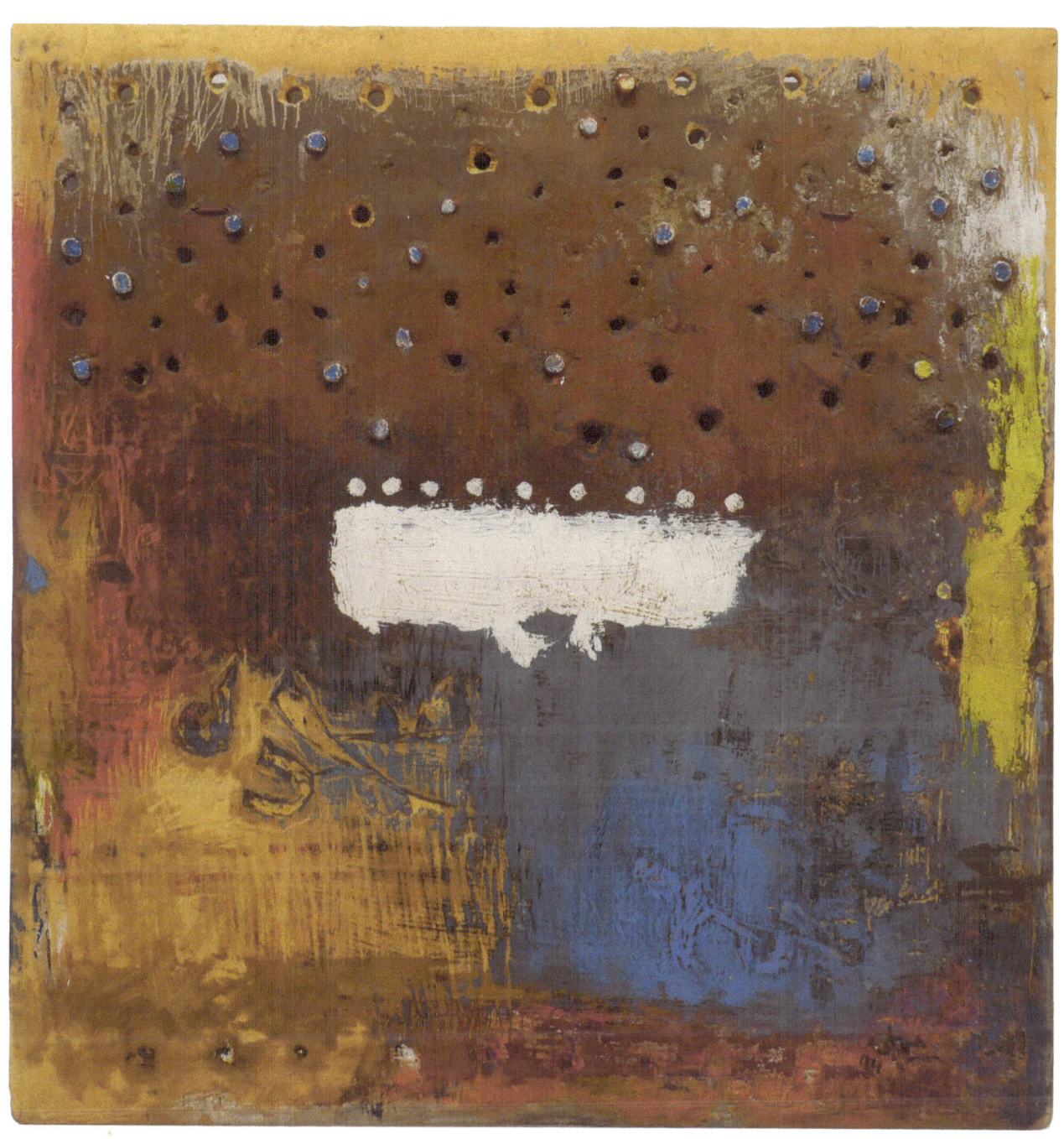

Plate 2

Hayder Ali

Black Talk, 2005

Mixed media on paper

9¼ x 13¼ in.

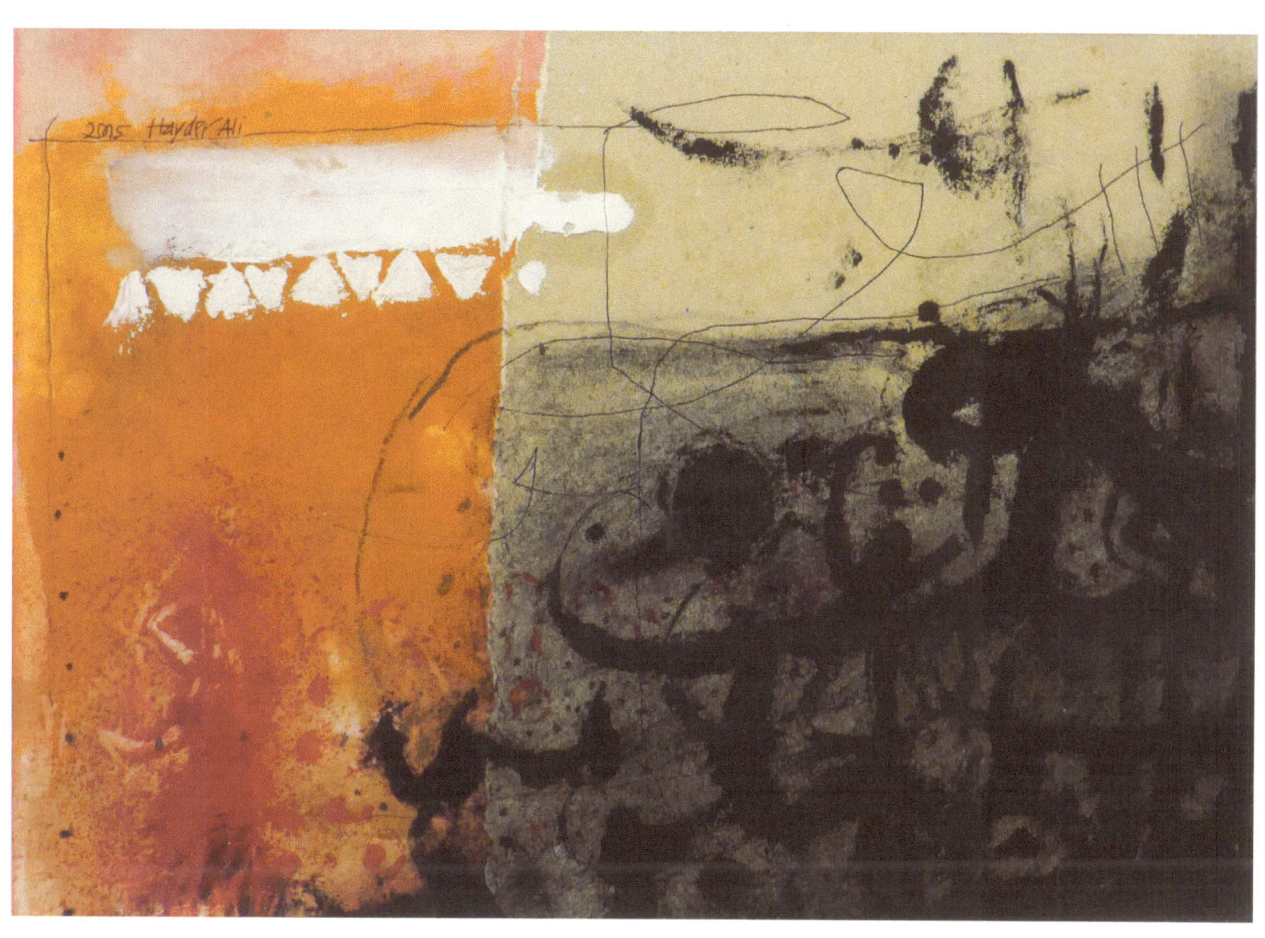

Plate 3

Hayder Ali

America, 2005

Mixed media on paper

9¼ x 13¼ in.

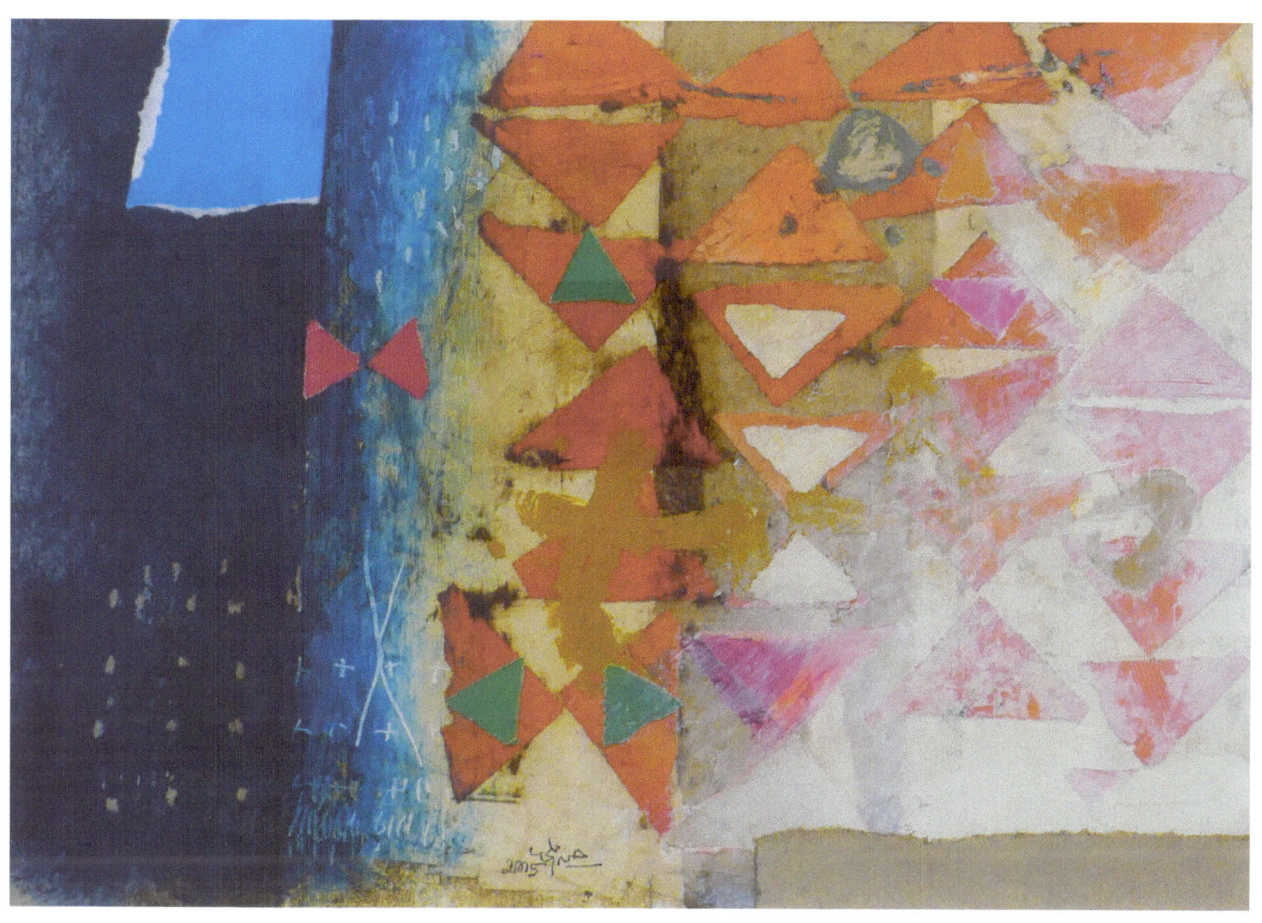

Plate 4

Hayder Ali

Memory Wall, 2006

Mixed media on paper

10¼ x 14 in.

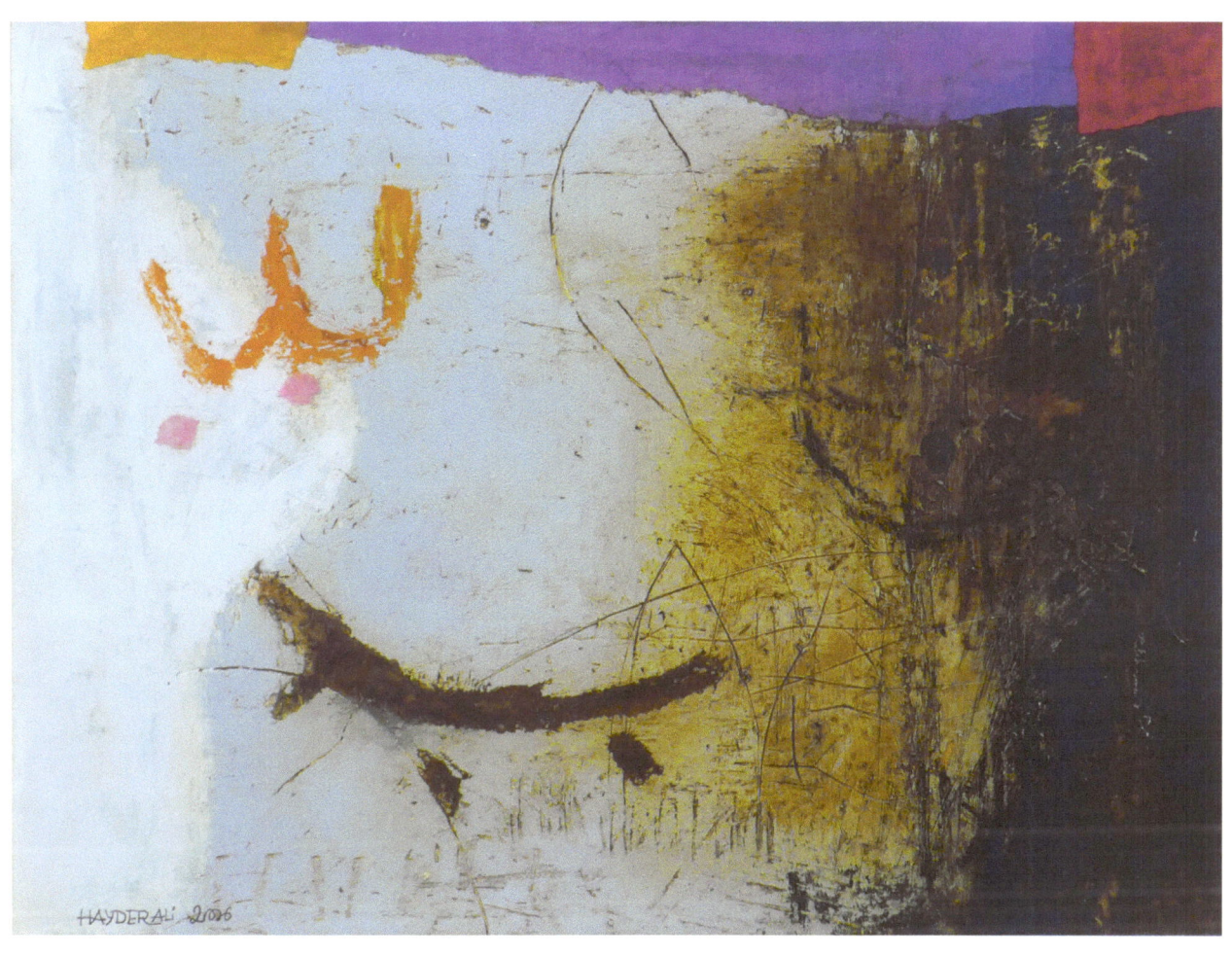

Plate 5

Hayder Ali

Elite, 2007

Mixed media on cardboard

10¼ x 14 in.

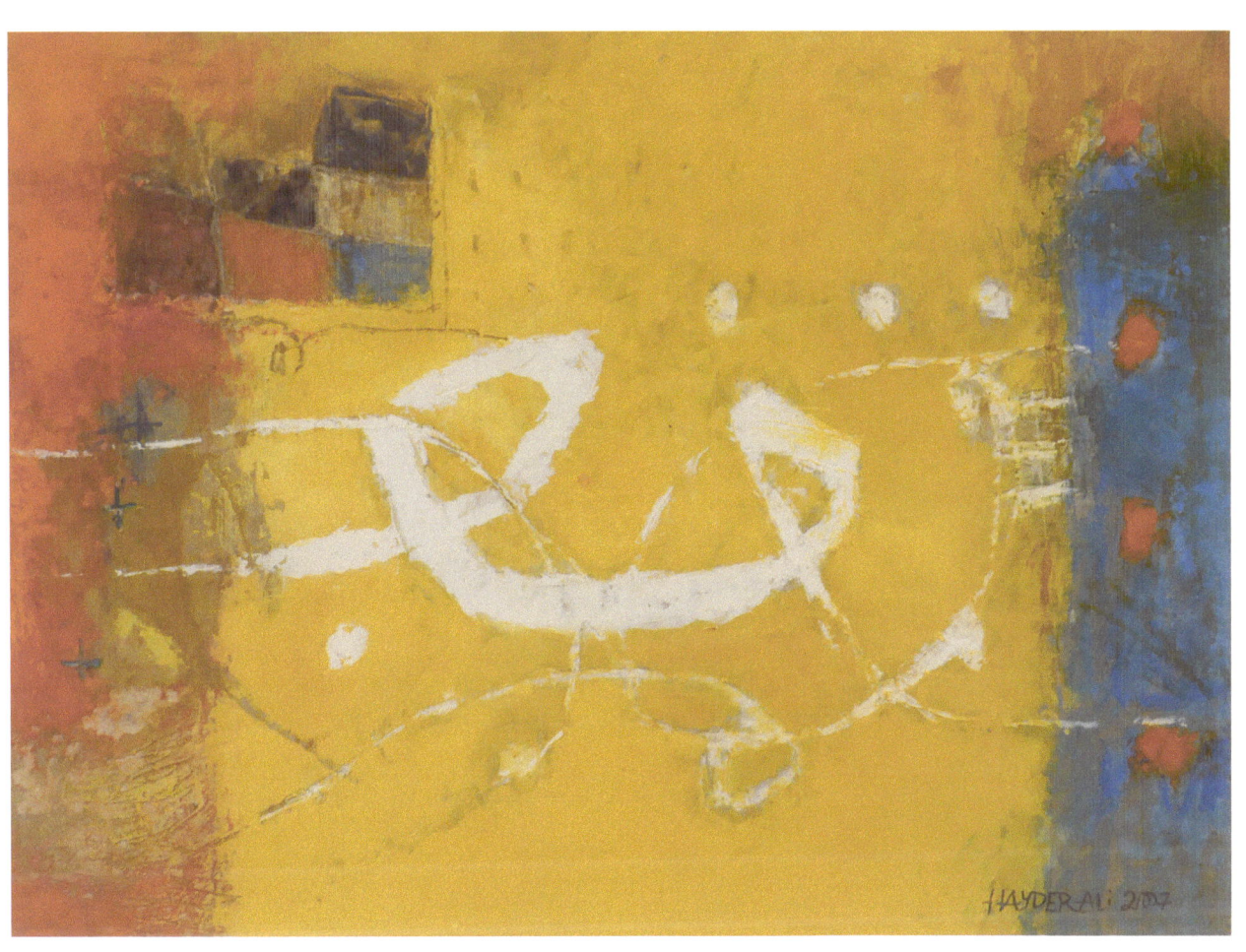

Plate 6

Amal Alwan

Basrah, n.d.

Oil on canvas

25 x 17 in.

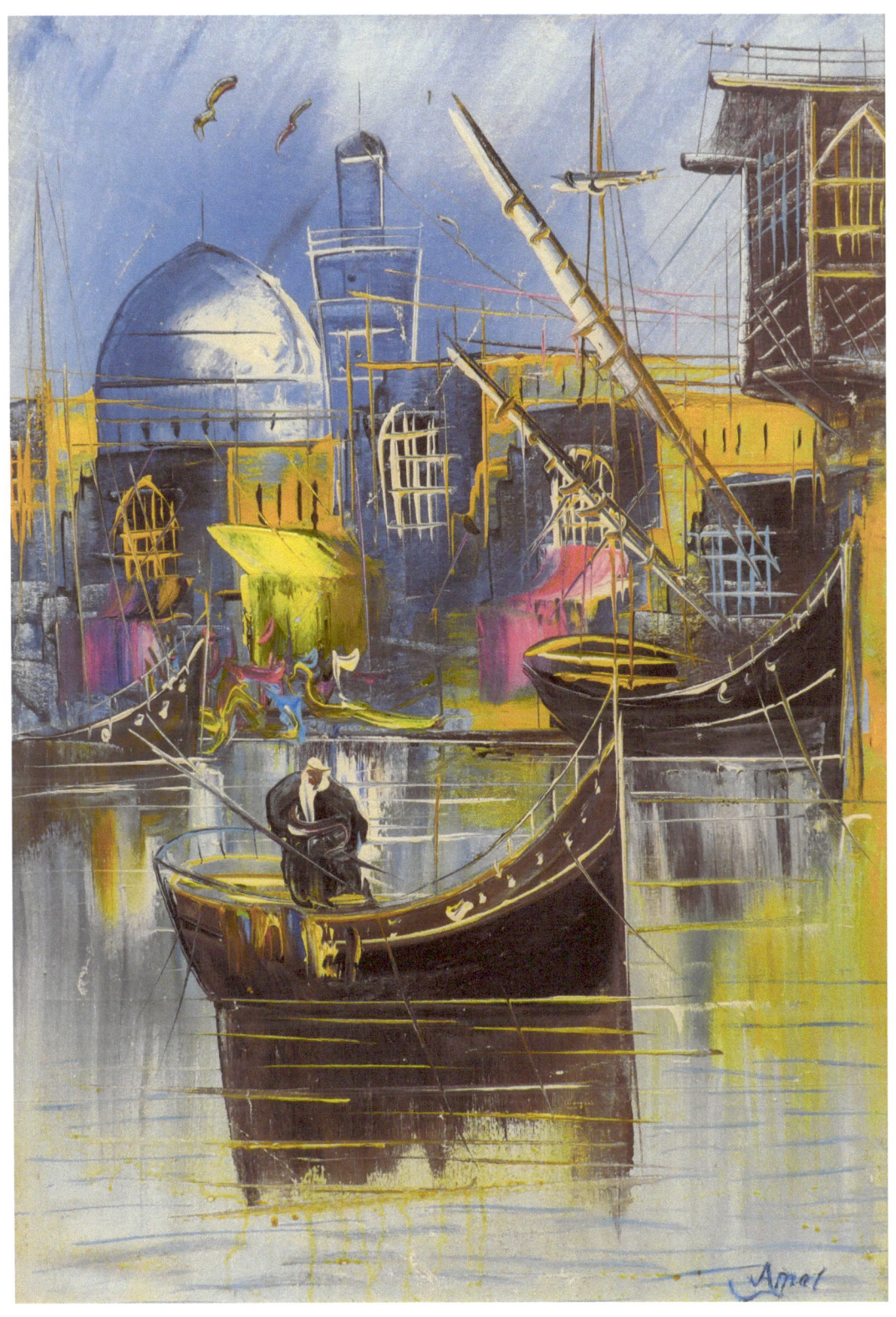

Plate 7

Amal Alwan

Blue Domed Mosque, n.d.

Oil on canvas

25½ x 17½ in.

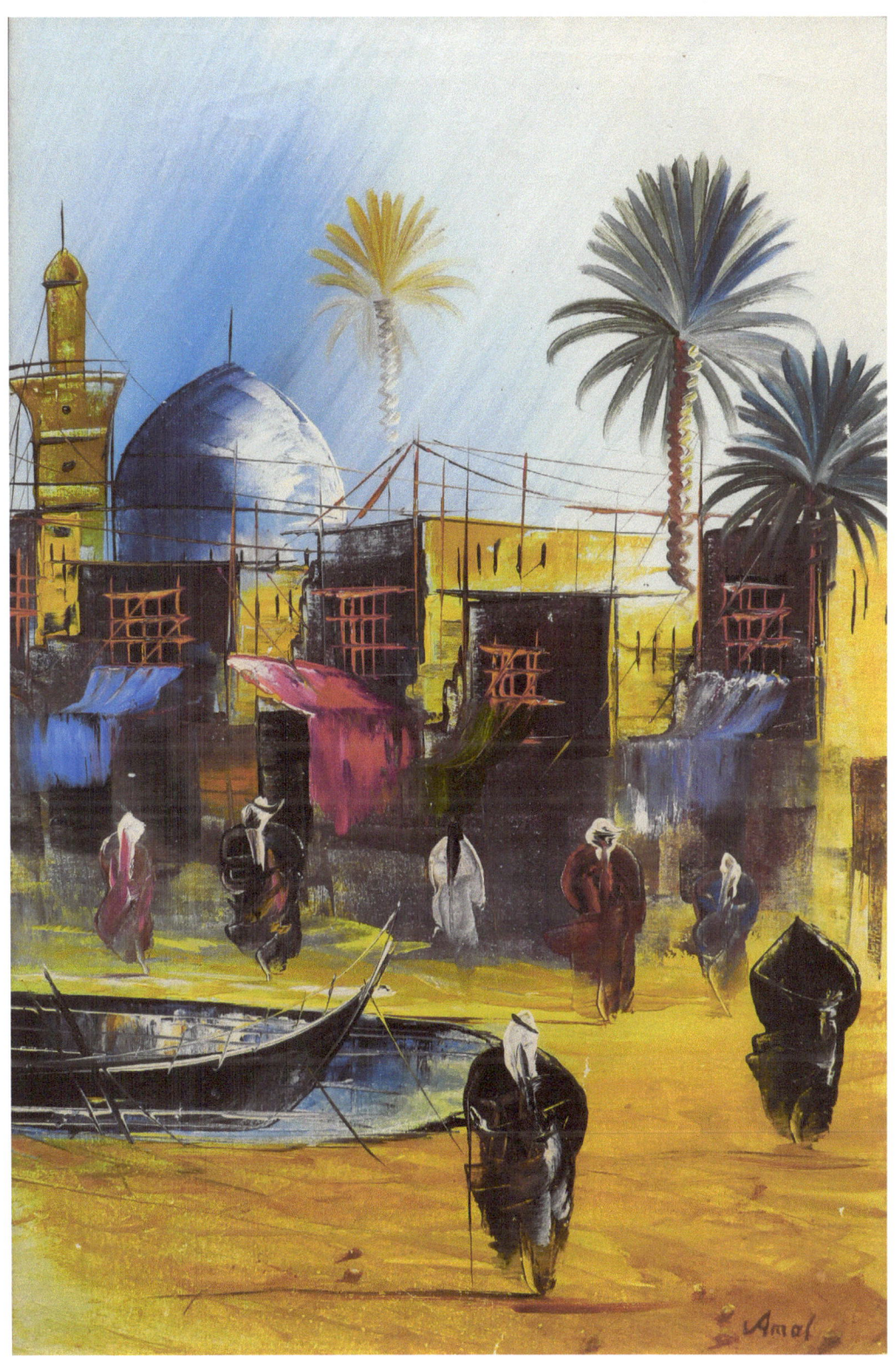

Plate 8

Oded Halahmy

Walking Home, 2004

Cast bronze

40½ x 29 x 11¾ in.

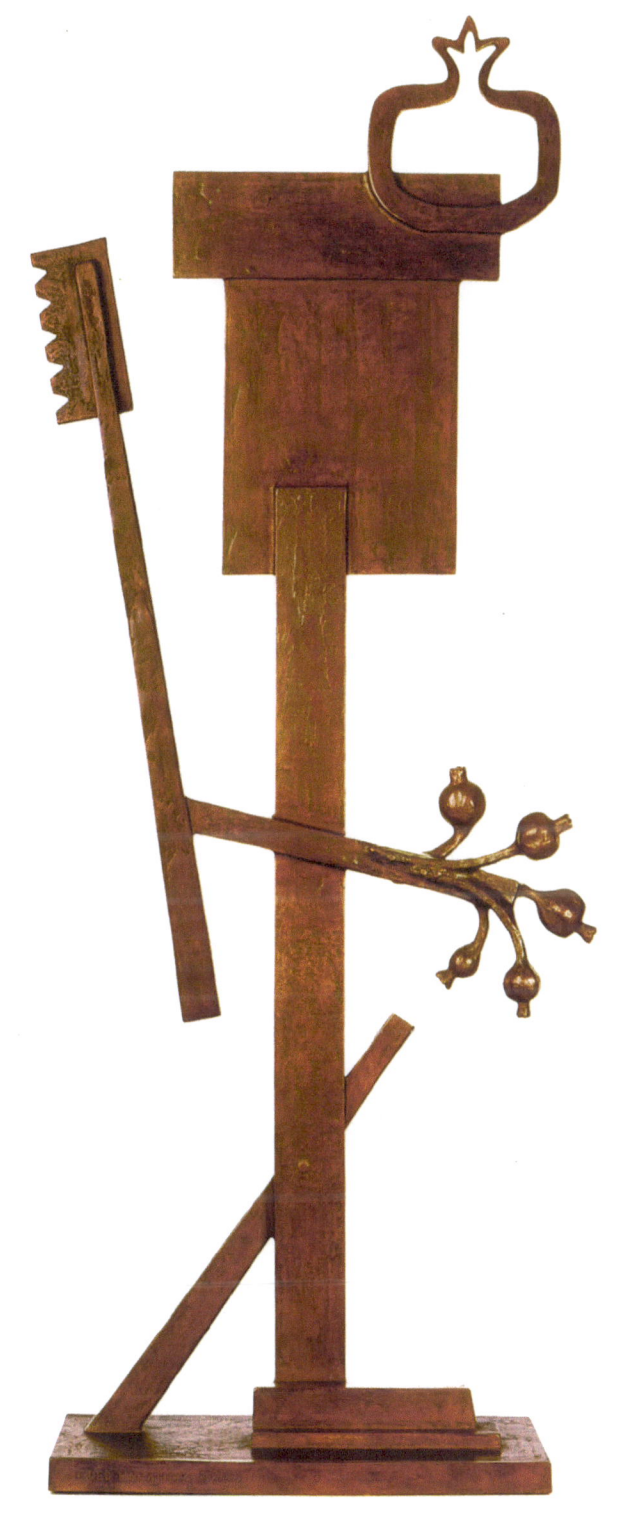

Plate 9

Oded Halahmy

Five Six Singing (Study), 2013

Cast bronze

20 x 6¾ x 6 in.

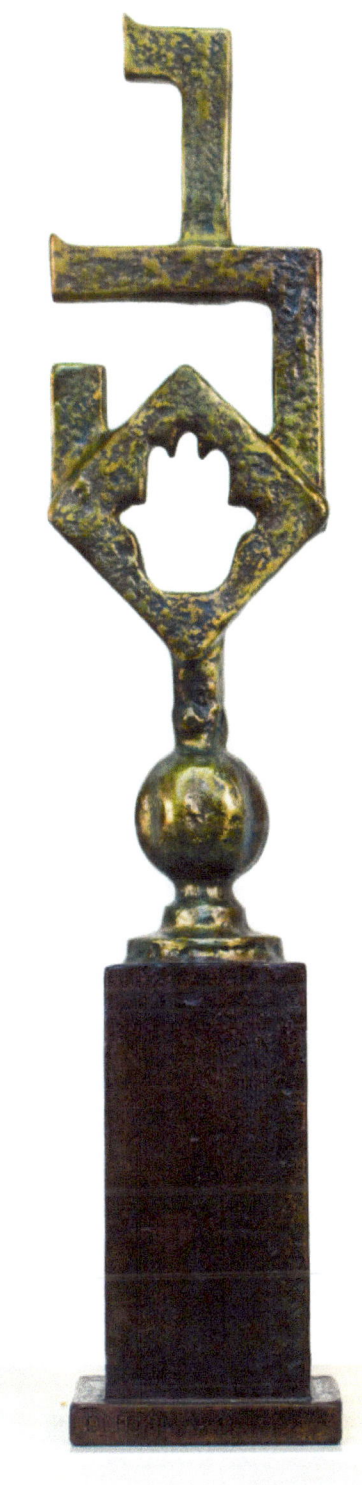

Plate 10

Oded Halahmy

Sing Hey Wow, 2013

Cast bronze, No. 208 (ed. 5)

32½ x 13¾ x 8½ in.

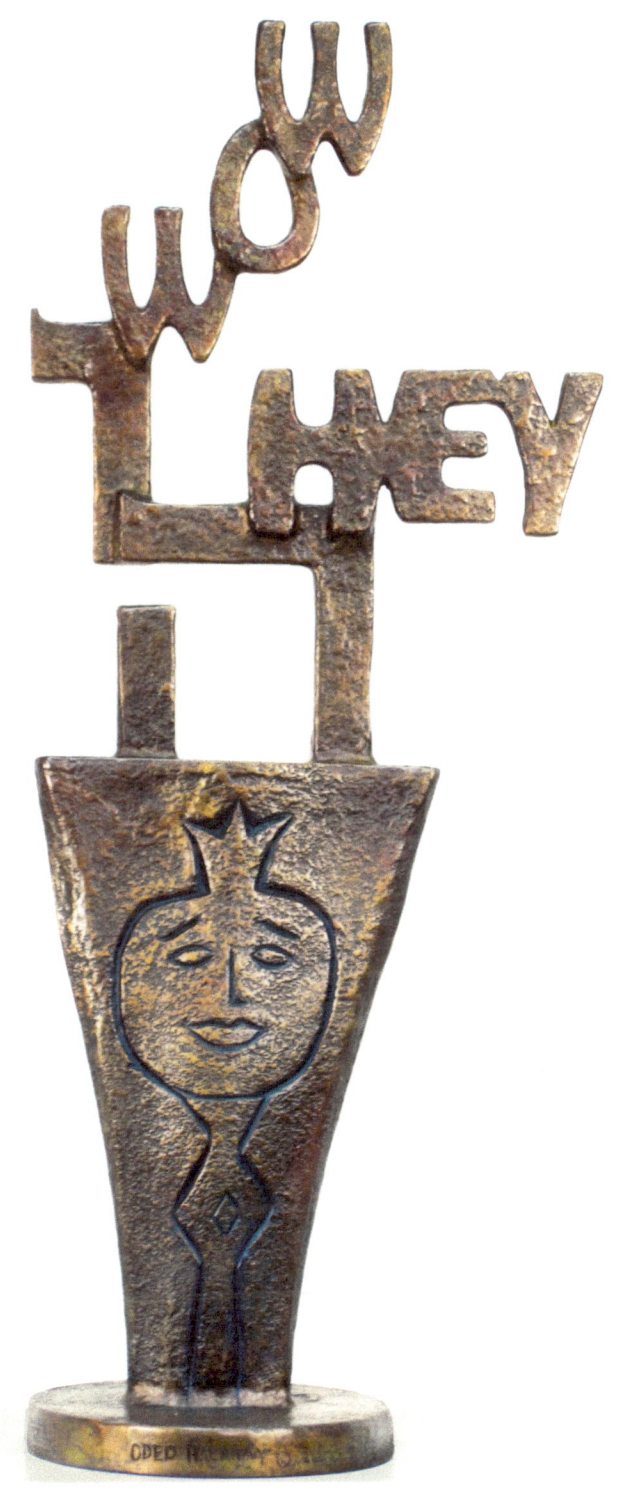

Plate 11

Oded Halahmy

Reading Hey Wow, 2013

Cast bronze

20 x 6¾ x 6 in.

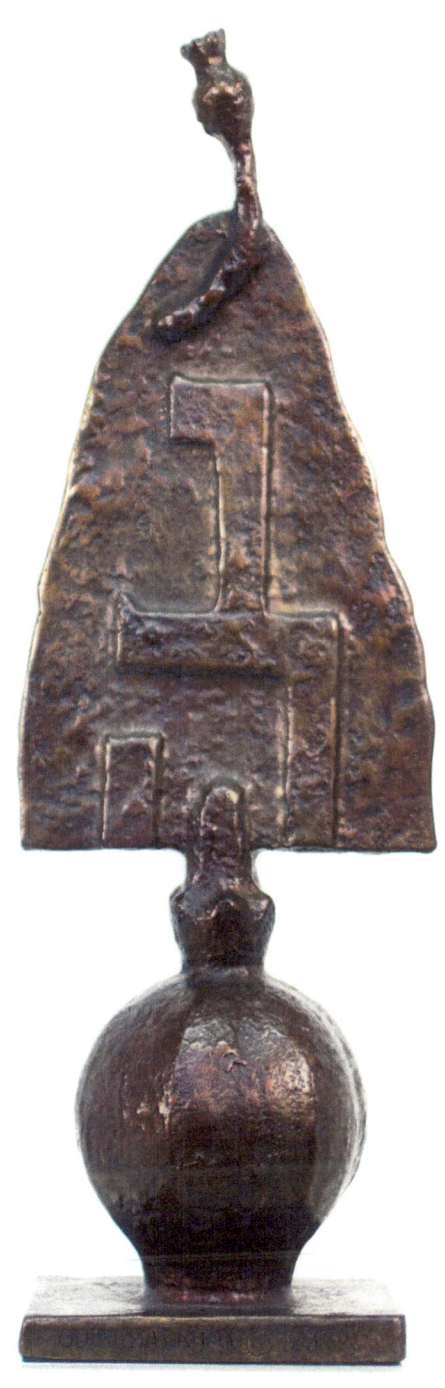

Plate 12

Mohammed al Hamadany

Untitled, from the series "Night of Fire (Laylat an Nar)," n.d.

Oil and acrylic on canvas

68 x 12½ in.

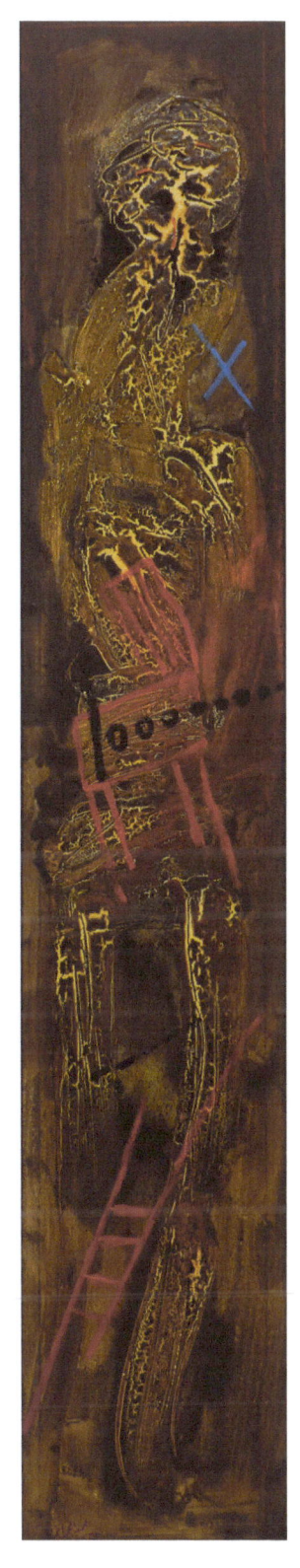

Plate 13

Mohammed al Hamadany

Untitled, from the series "Night of Fire (Laylat an Nar)," n.d.

Oil and acrylic on canvas

68 x 12½ in.

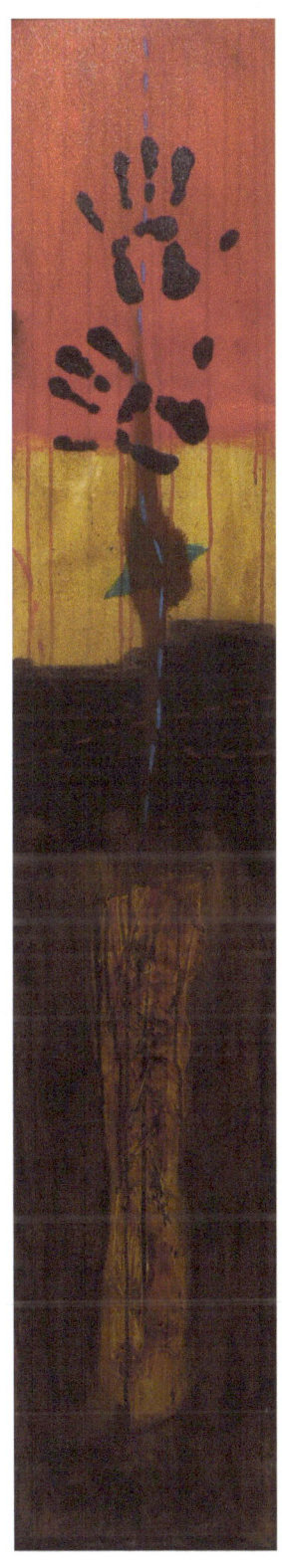

Plate 14

Ismail Khayat

Untitled, from the series "Anfal Memory," 2006
Ink and pigment on watercolor paper
11½ x 7½ in.

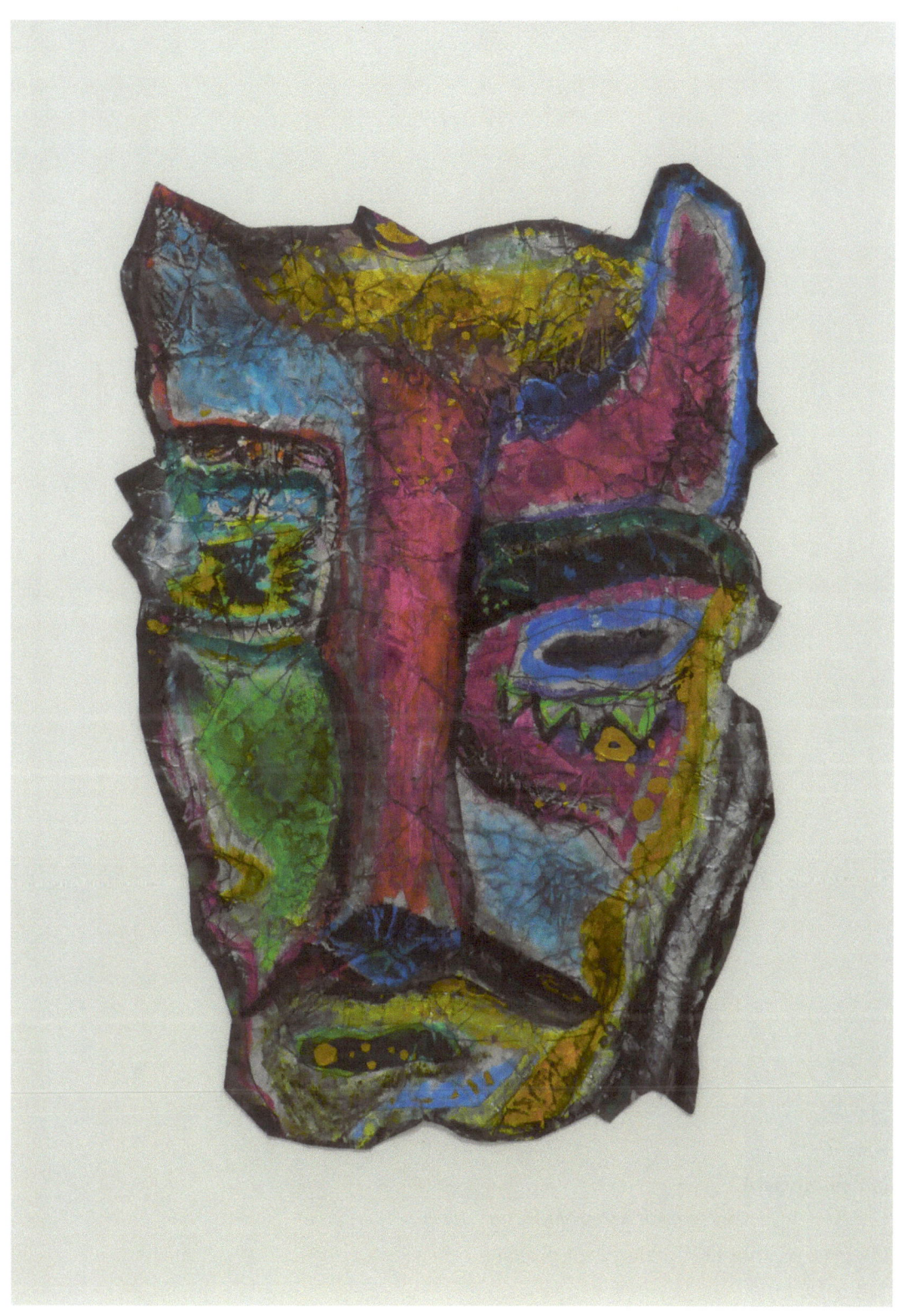

Plate 15

Ismail Khayat

Untitled, from the series "Anfal Memory," 2006
Ink and pigment on watercolor paper
11½ x 7½ in.

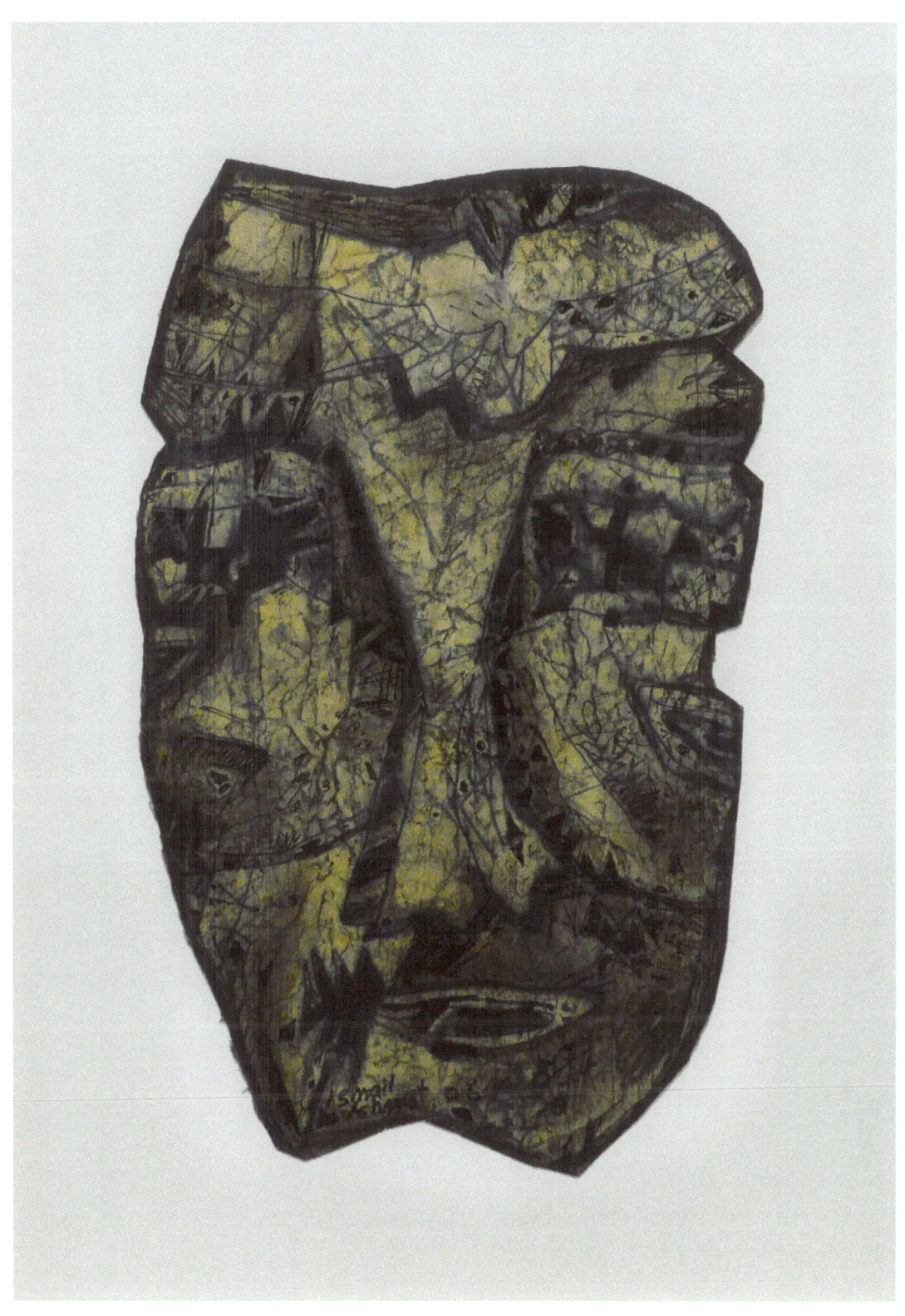

Plate 16

Ismail Khayat

Untitled, from the series "Anfal Memory," 2006
Ink and pigment on watercolor paper
11½ x 7½ in.

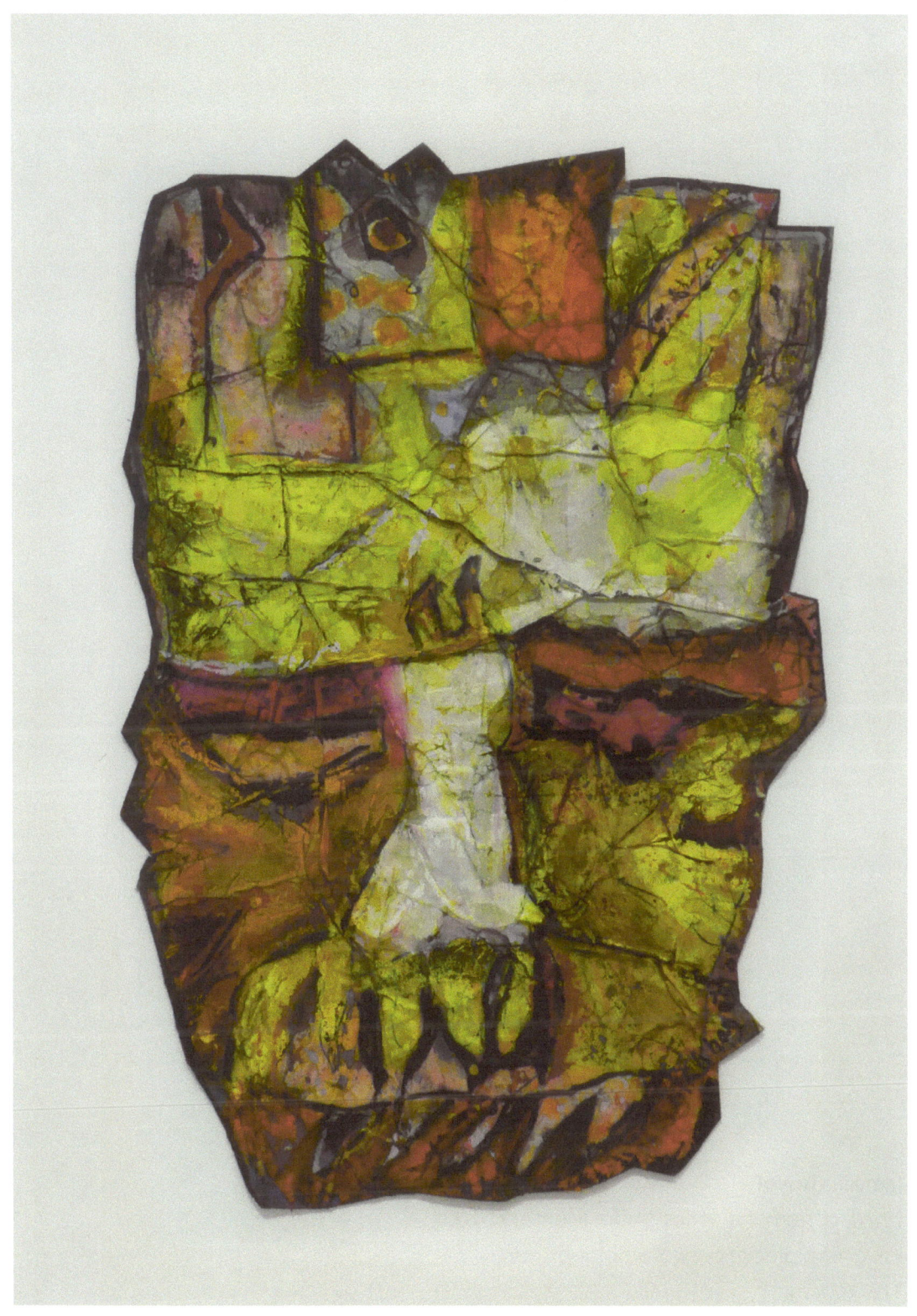

Plate 17

Ismail Khayat

Untitled, from the series "Anfal Memory," 2006
Ink and pigment on watercolor paper
11½ x 7½ in.

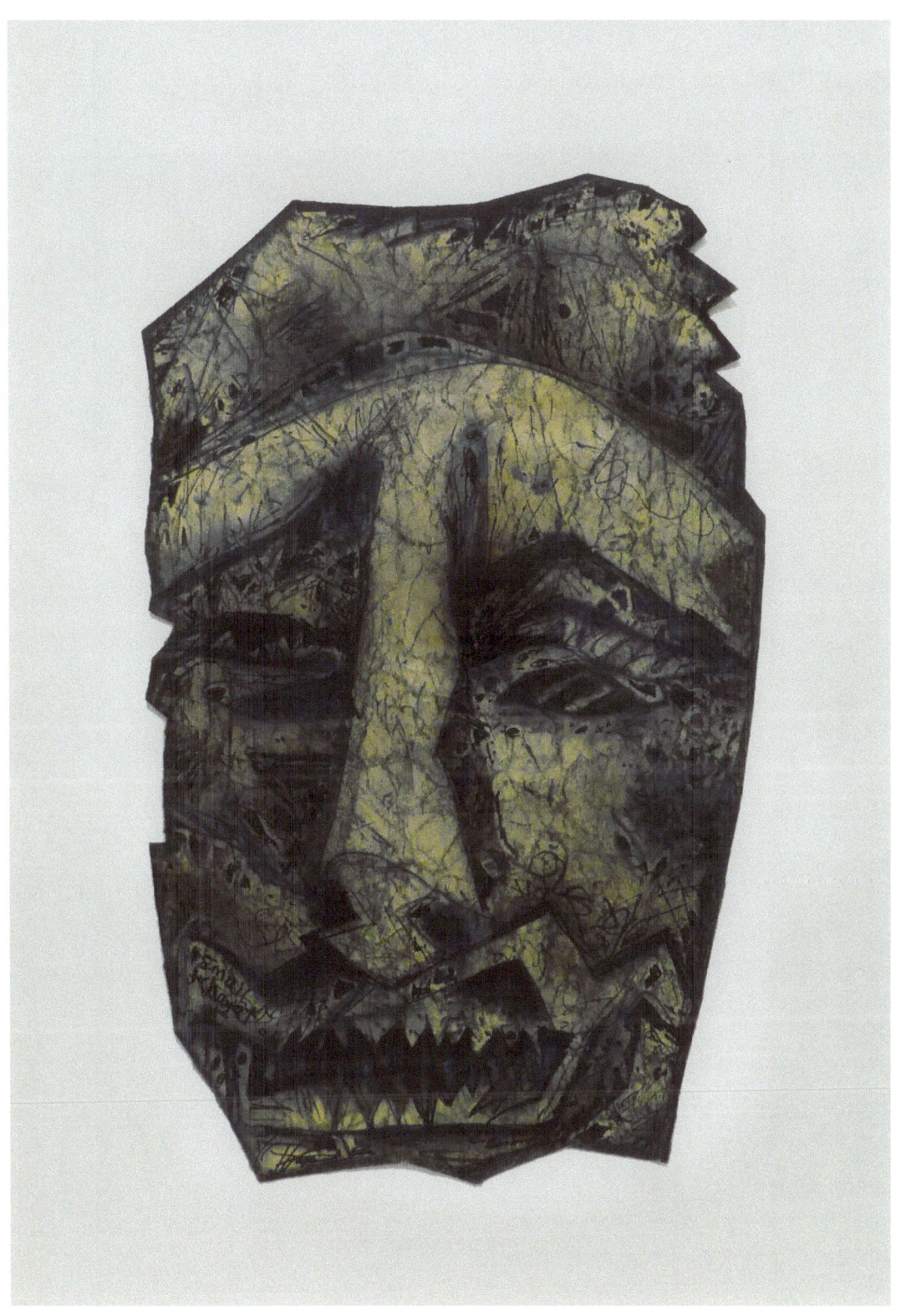

Plate 18

Ismail Khayat

Untitled, from the series "Anfal Memory," 2006

Ink and pigment on watercolor paper

11½ x 7½ in.

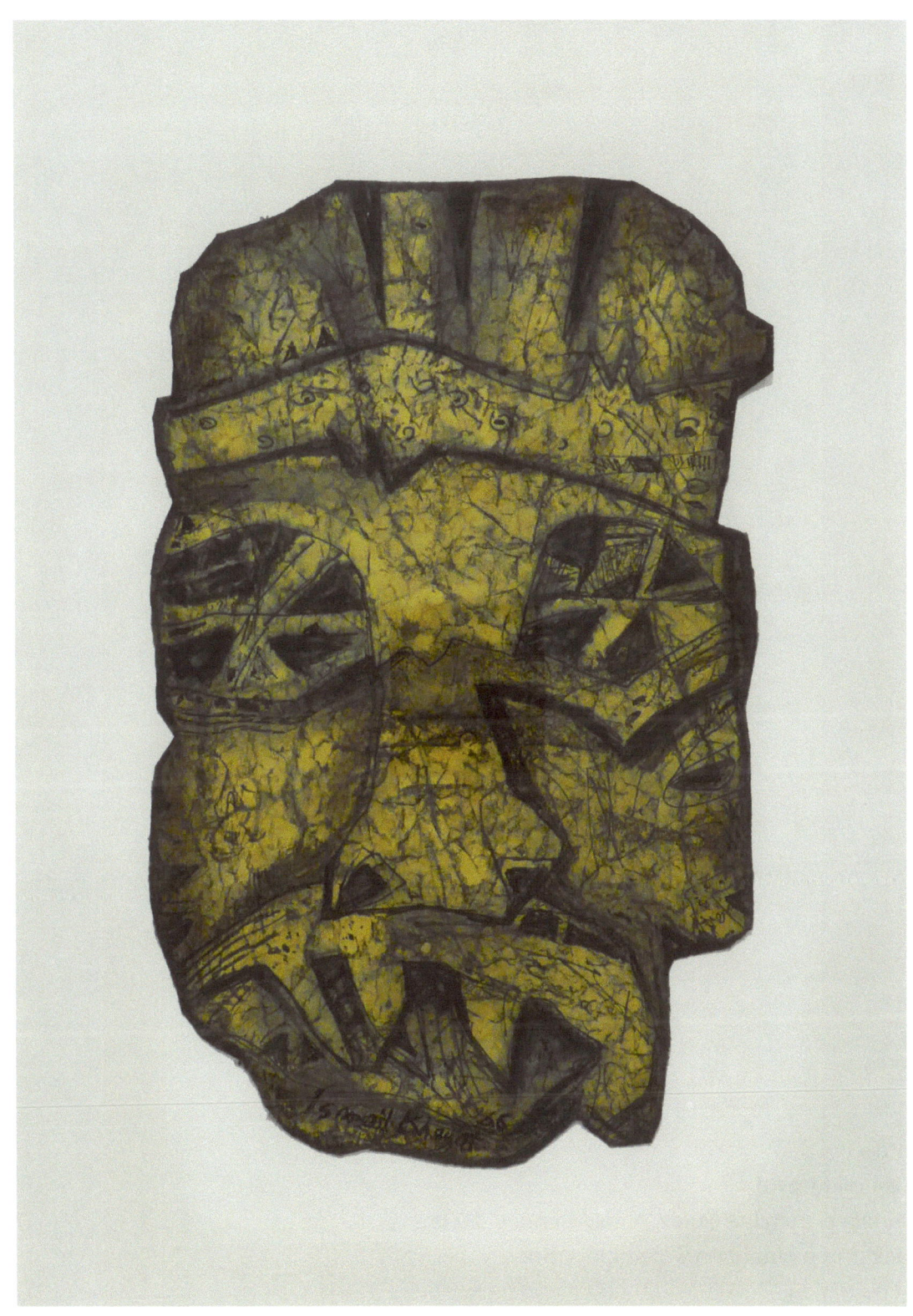

Plate 19

Ismail Khayat

Untitled, from the series "Anfal Memory," 2006

Ink and pigment on watercolor paper

11½ x 7½ in.

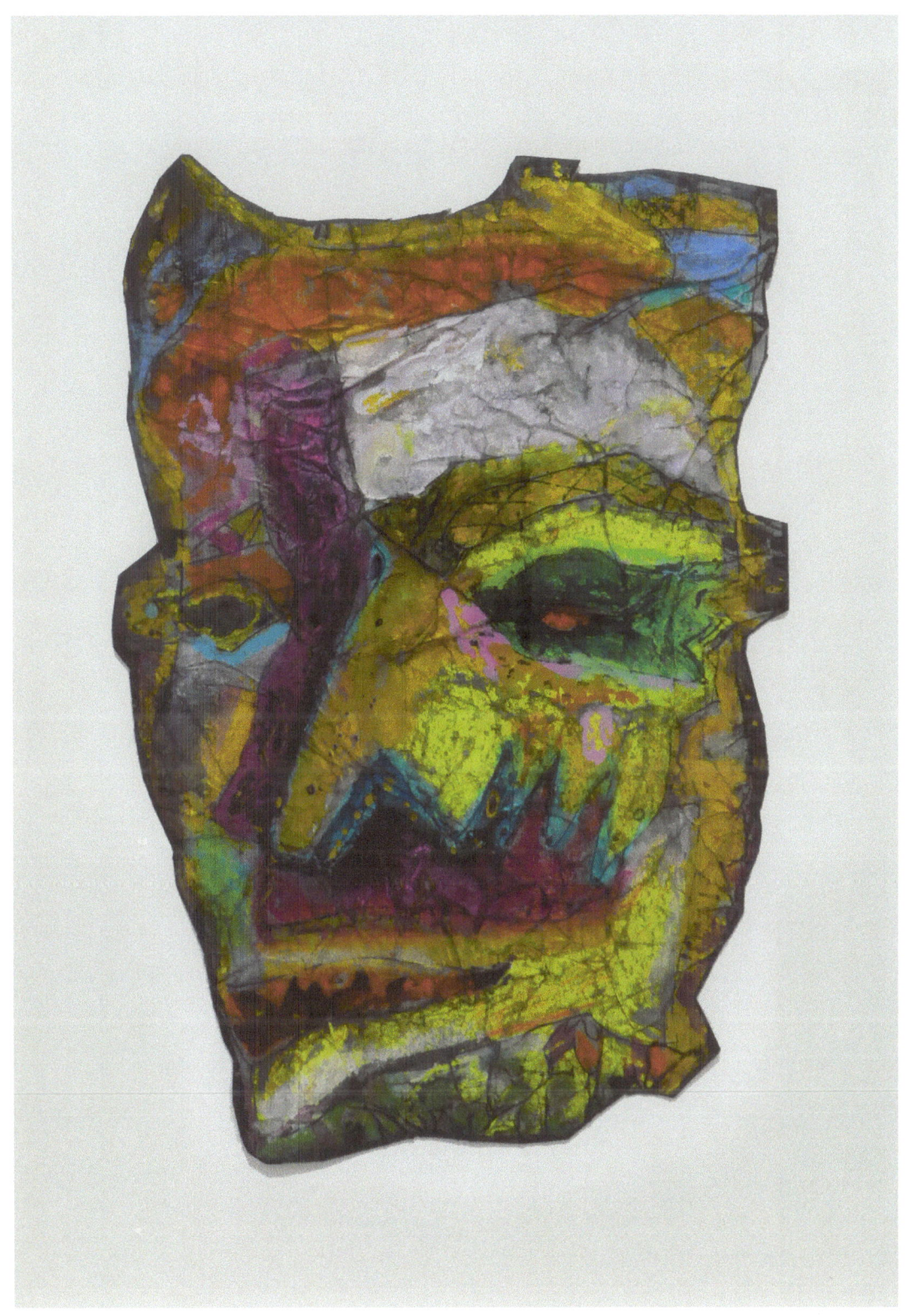

Plate 20

Hanaa Malallah

Uruk Old Love, 2006

Mixed media on carved wood

15½ x 15½ in.

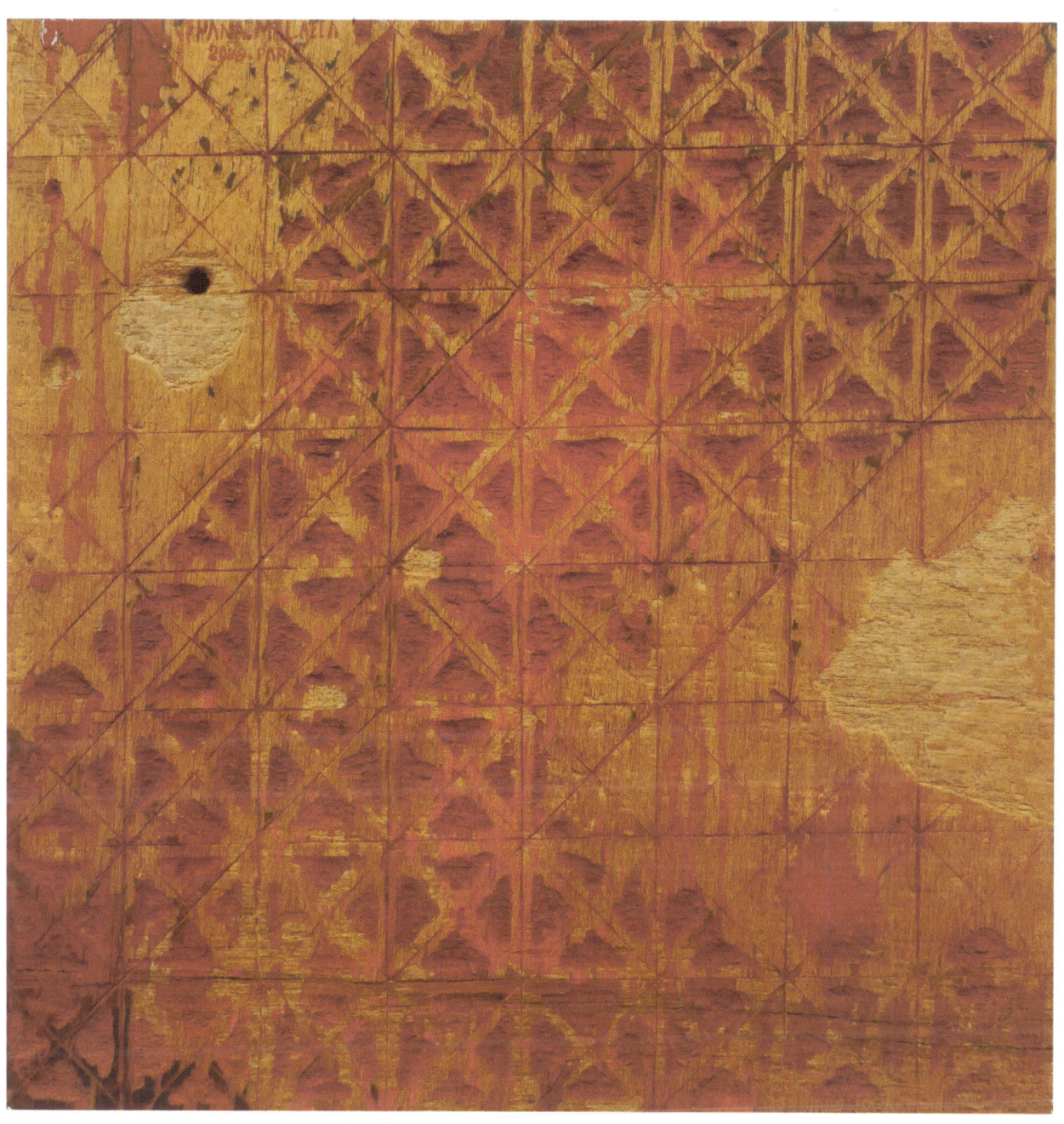

65

Plate 21

Hanaa Malallah

Uruk Wall, 2006

Mixed media on carved wood

15½ x 15½ in.

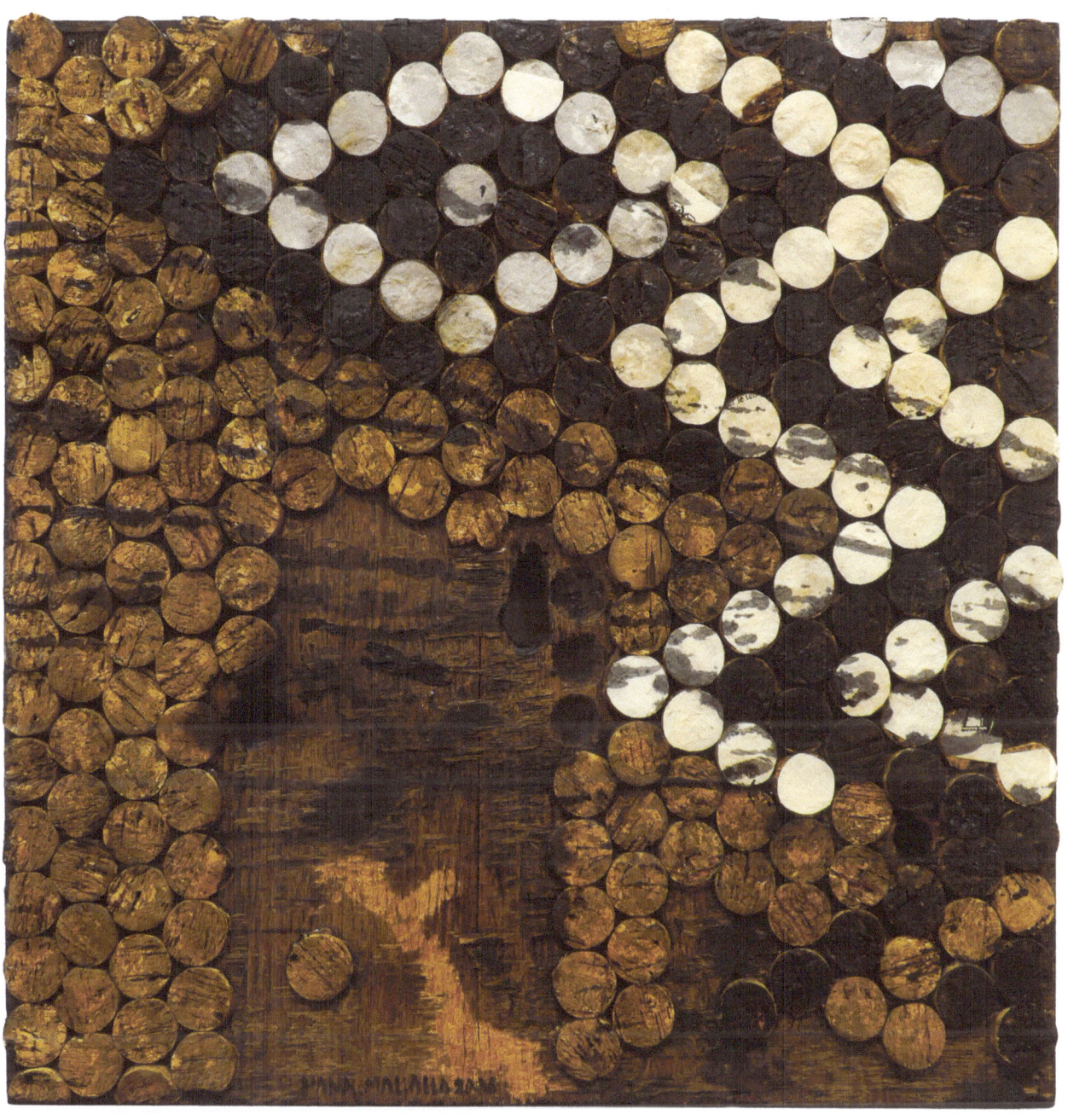

Plate 22

Hassan Massoudy

Sur terre, il y a place pour tous, Schiller, 2006
Water-based pigments on paper
29½ x 21¾ in.

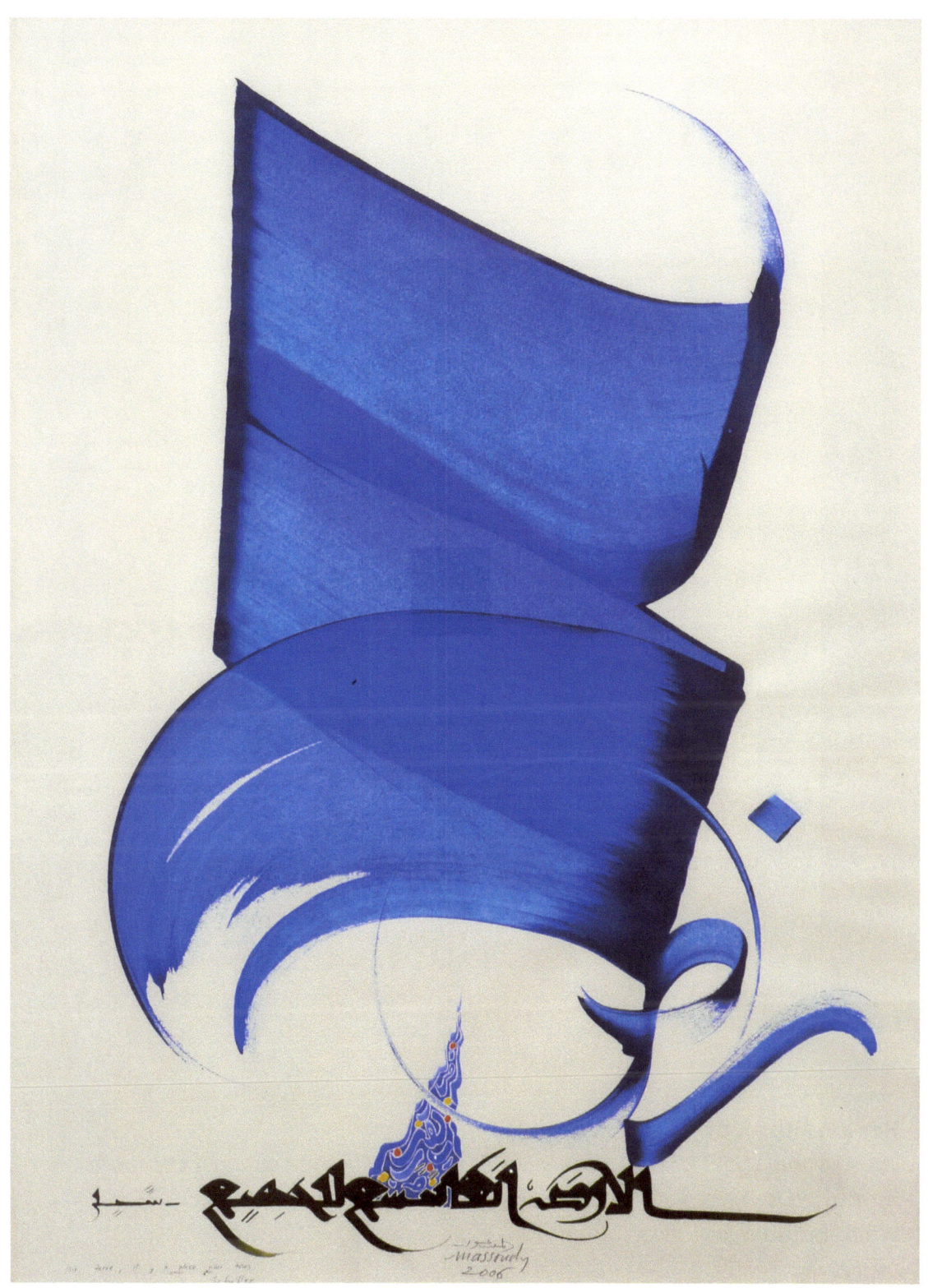

Plate 23

Hassan Massoudy

*The love that I hold for you, that is my eternal delight / The passion that I swear
to you, this is my religion, Ibn Zaydoun 11th century,* 2008
Water-based pigments on paper
29 x 23 in.

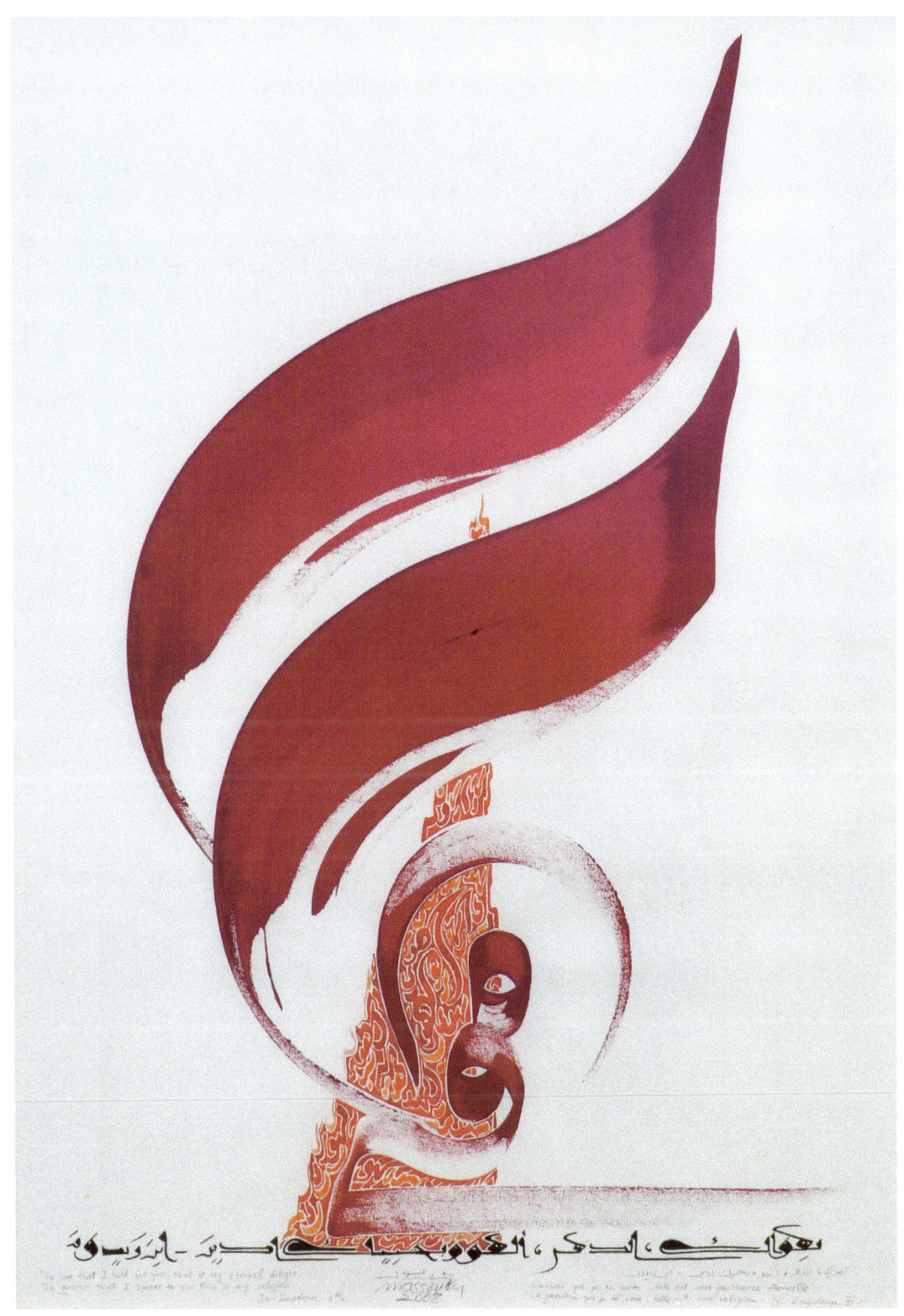

Plate 24

Naziha Rashid

Woman in the Village, 1999

Watercolor and gouache on paper

14 x 11 in.

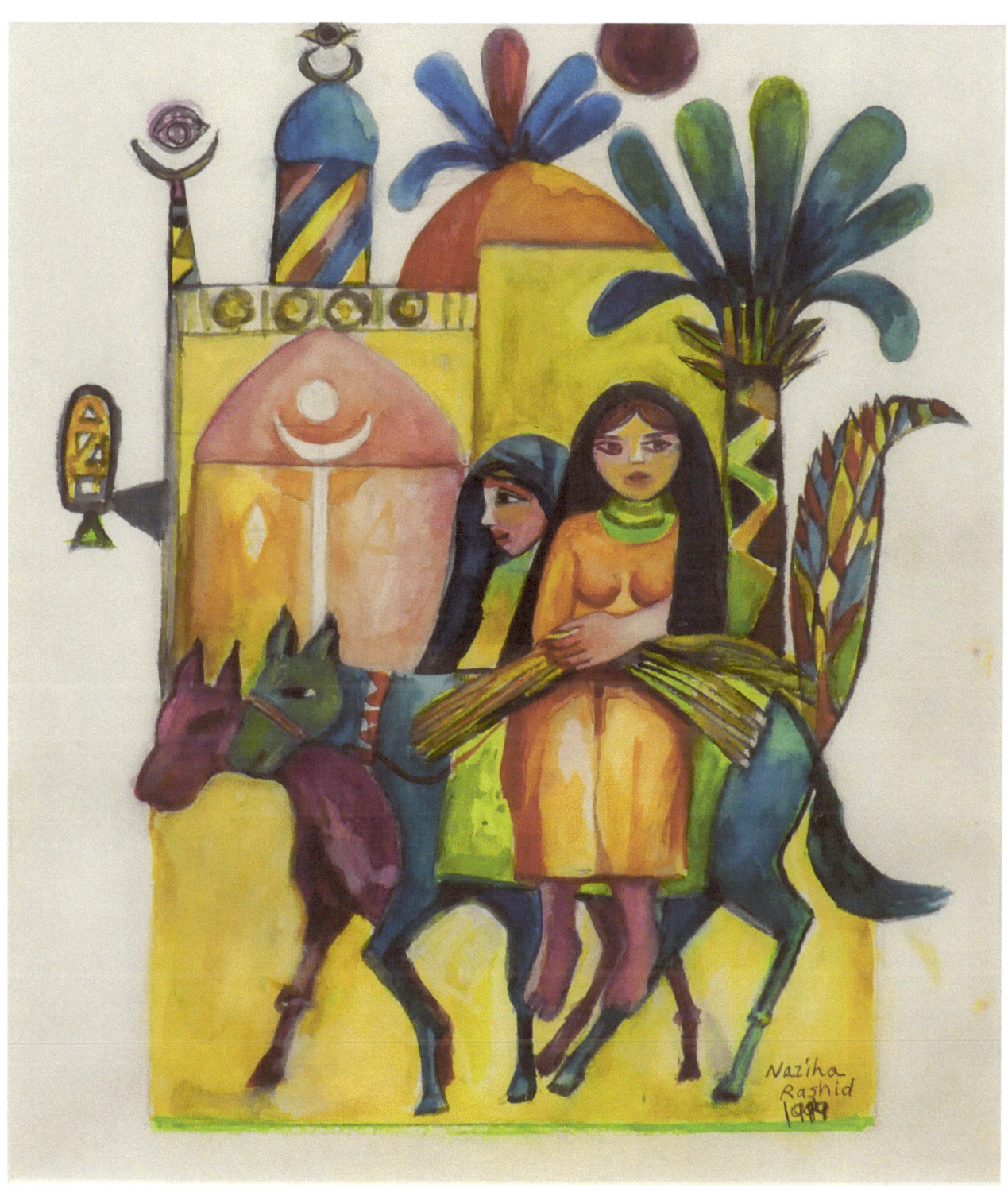

Plate 25

Naziha Rashid

Nostalgic, 2000

Acrylic on canvas

19 x 16 in.

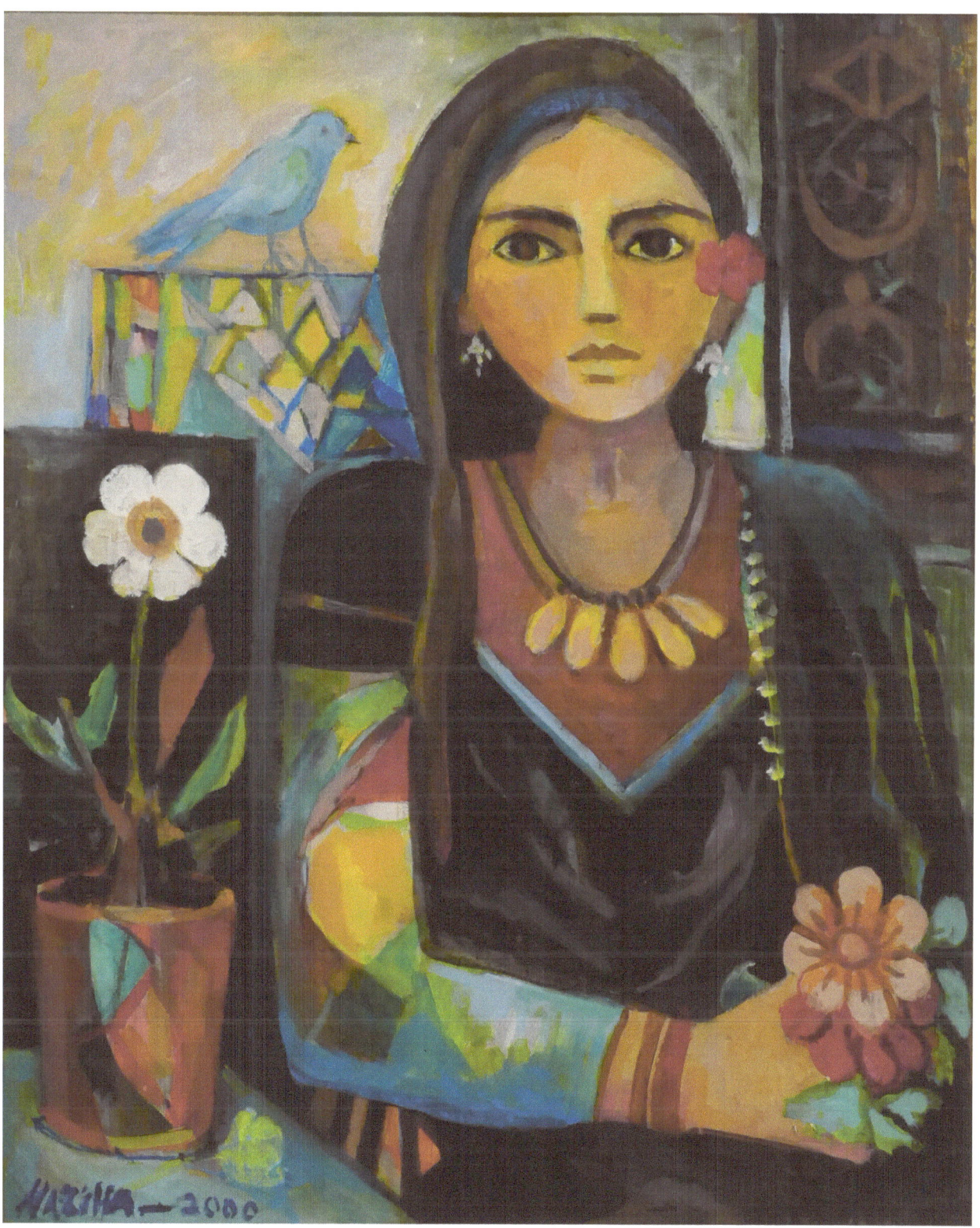

Plate 26

Naziha Rashid

Evil Eye, 2003

Watercolor, gouache, and ink on paper

8½ x 11 in.

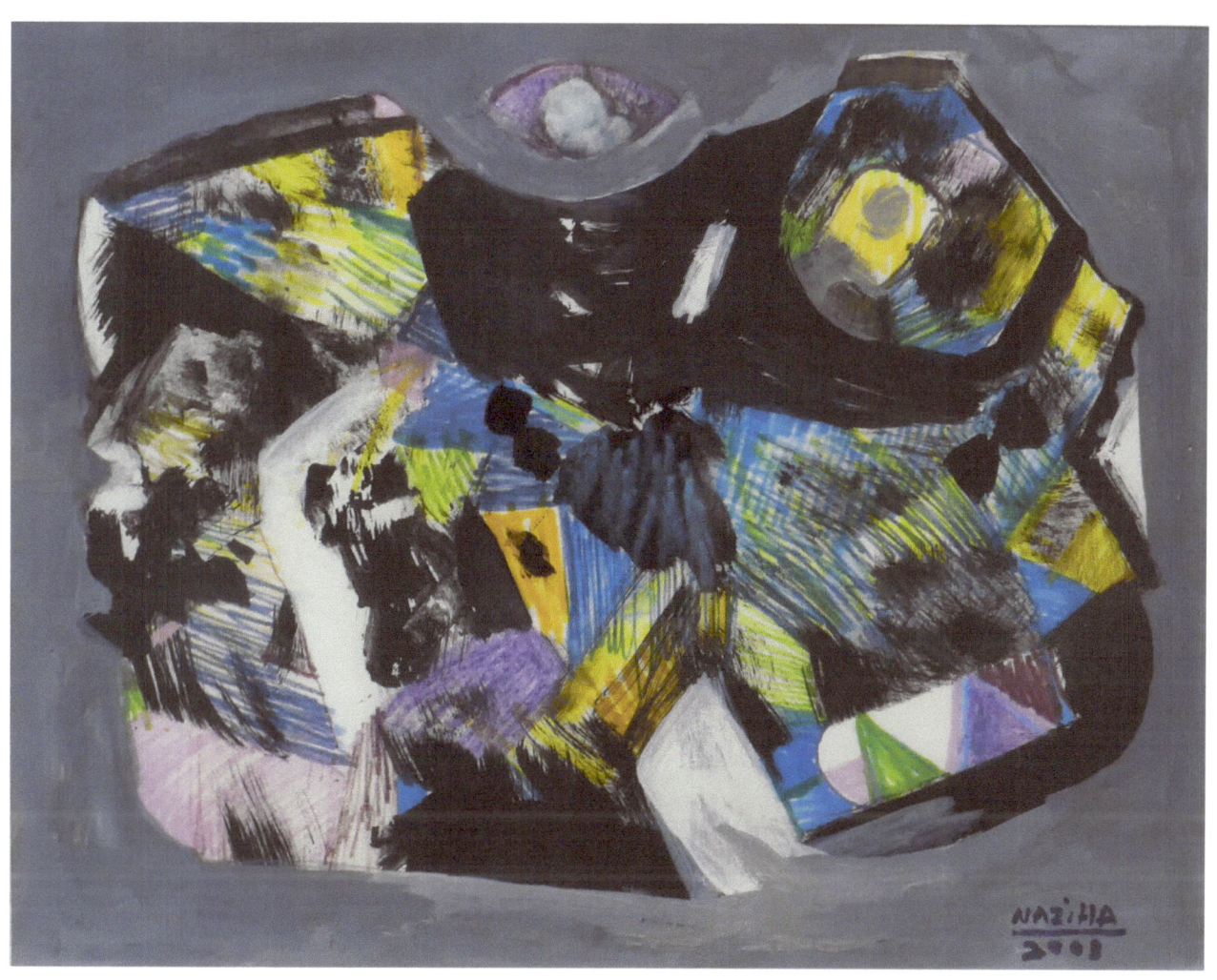

Plate 27

Naziha Rashid

In the Market, 2006

Watercolor and acrylic on paper

13 x 19 in.

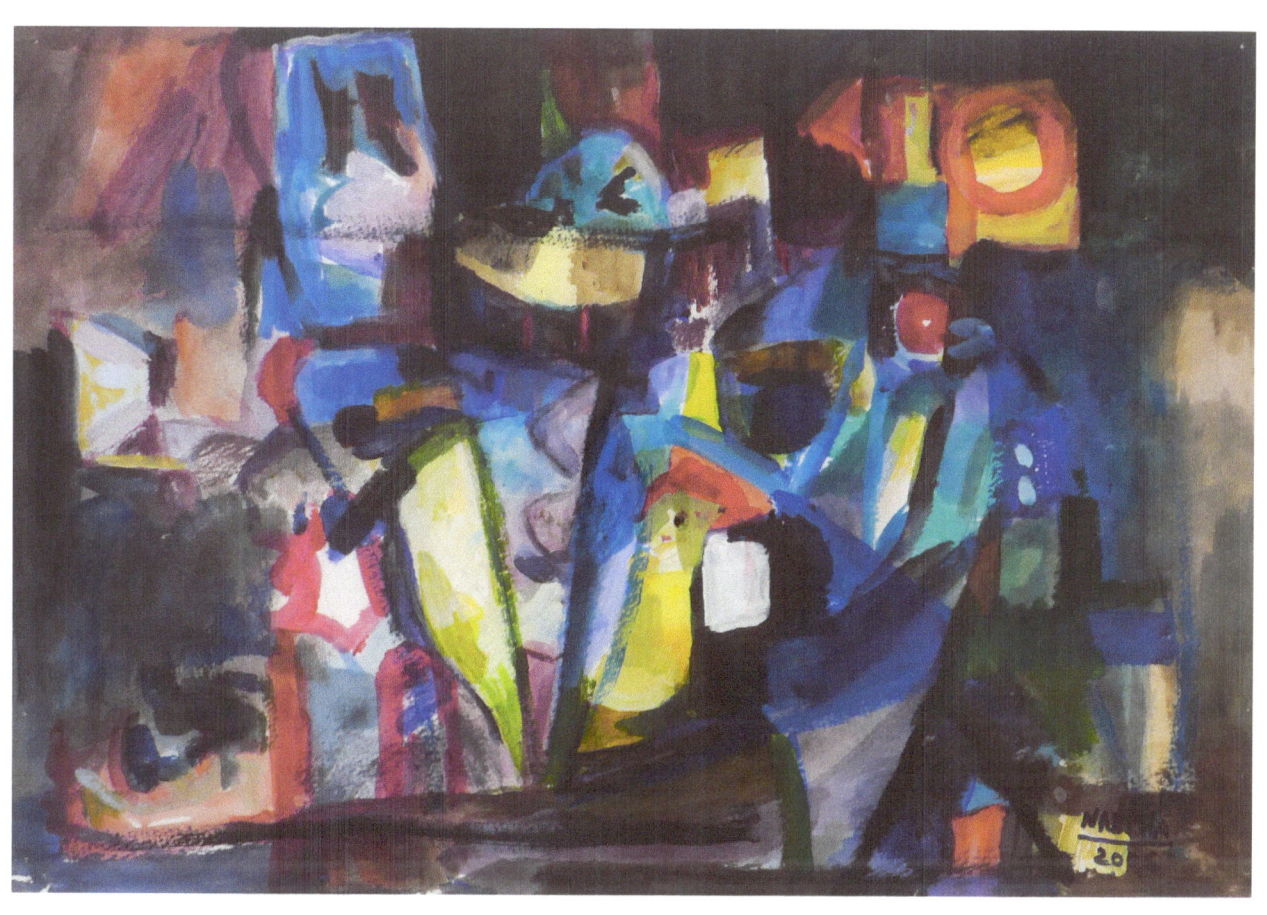

Plate 28

Qasim Sabti

Untitled, from the series "Book Cover Collage," n.d.

Book cover and collage

15¼ x 9½ in.

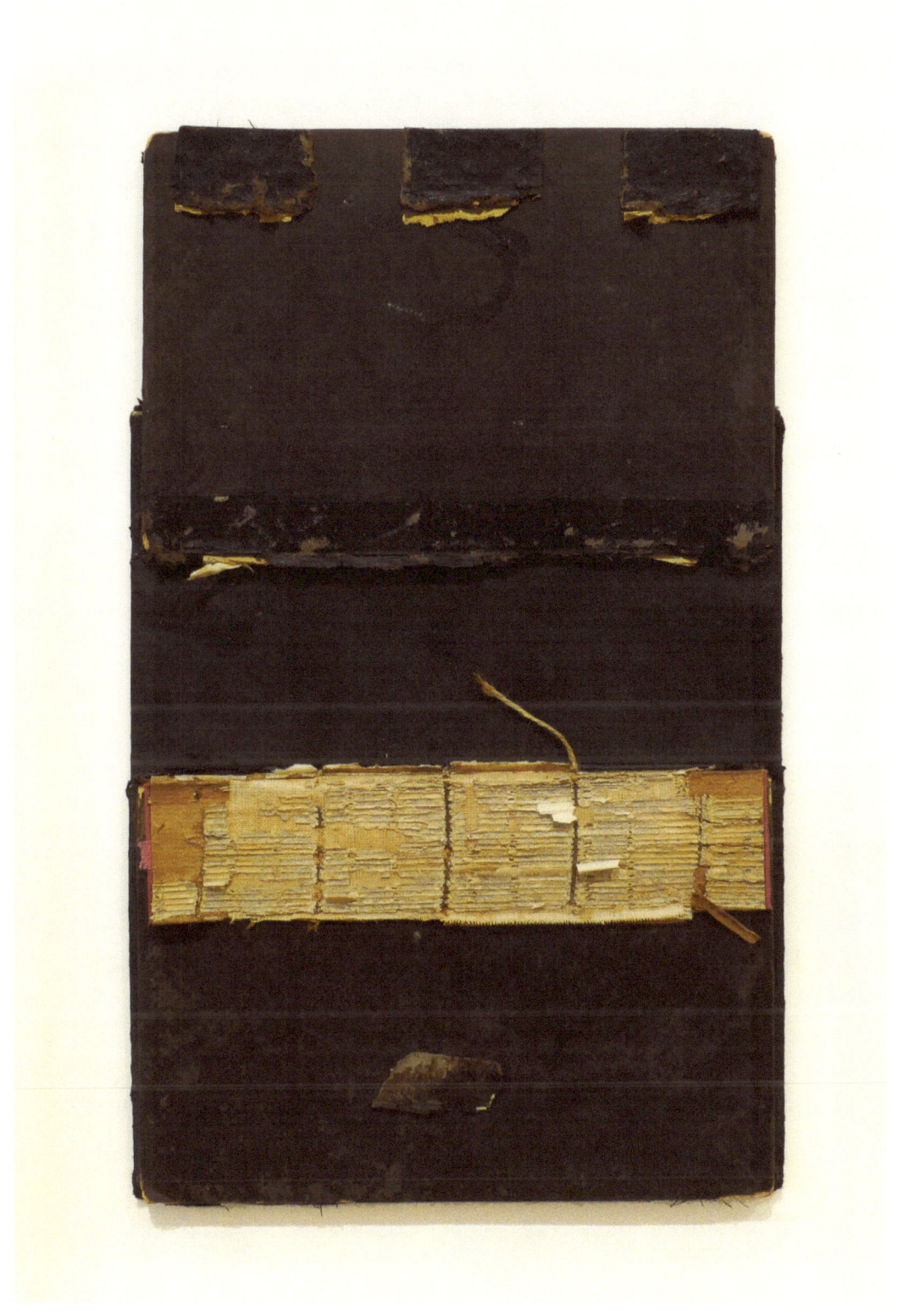

Plate 29

Qasim Sabti

Untitled, from the series "Book Cover Collage," 2006

Book cover and collage

12½ x 8½ in.

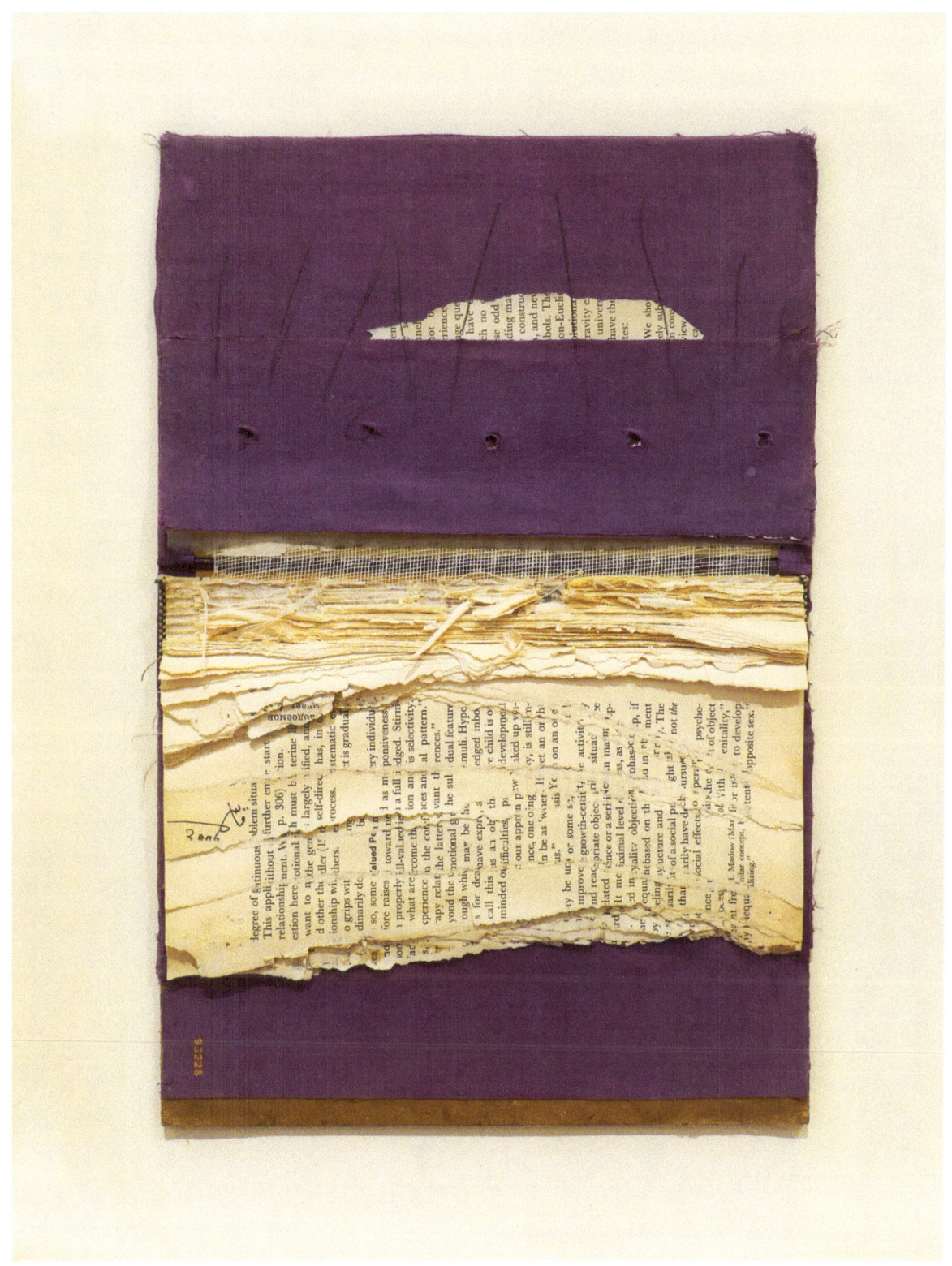

Plate 30

Qasim Sabti

Untitled, from the series "Book Cover Collage," 2006

Book cover and collage

14⅞ x 8¾ in.

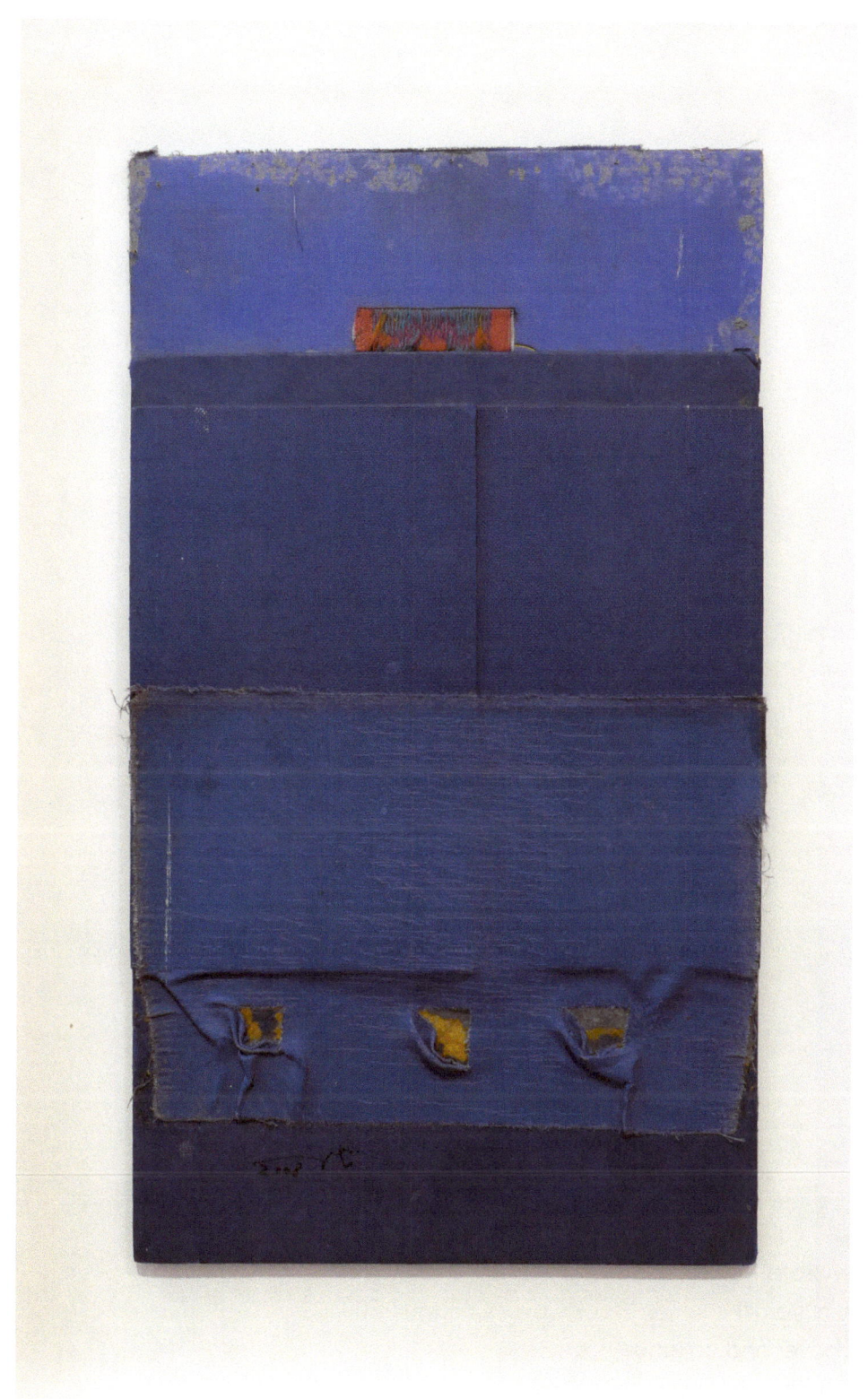

Plate 31

Qasim Sabti

Untitled, from the series "Book Cover Collage," 2008

Book cover and collage

18¾ x 8¼ in.

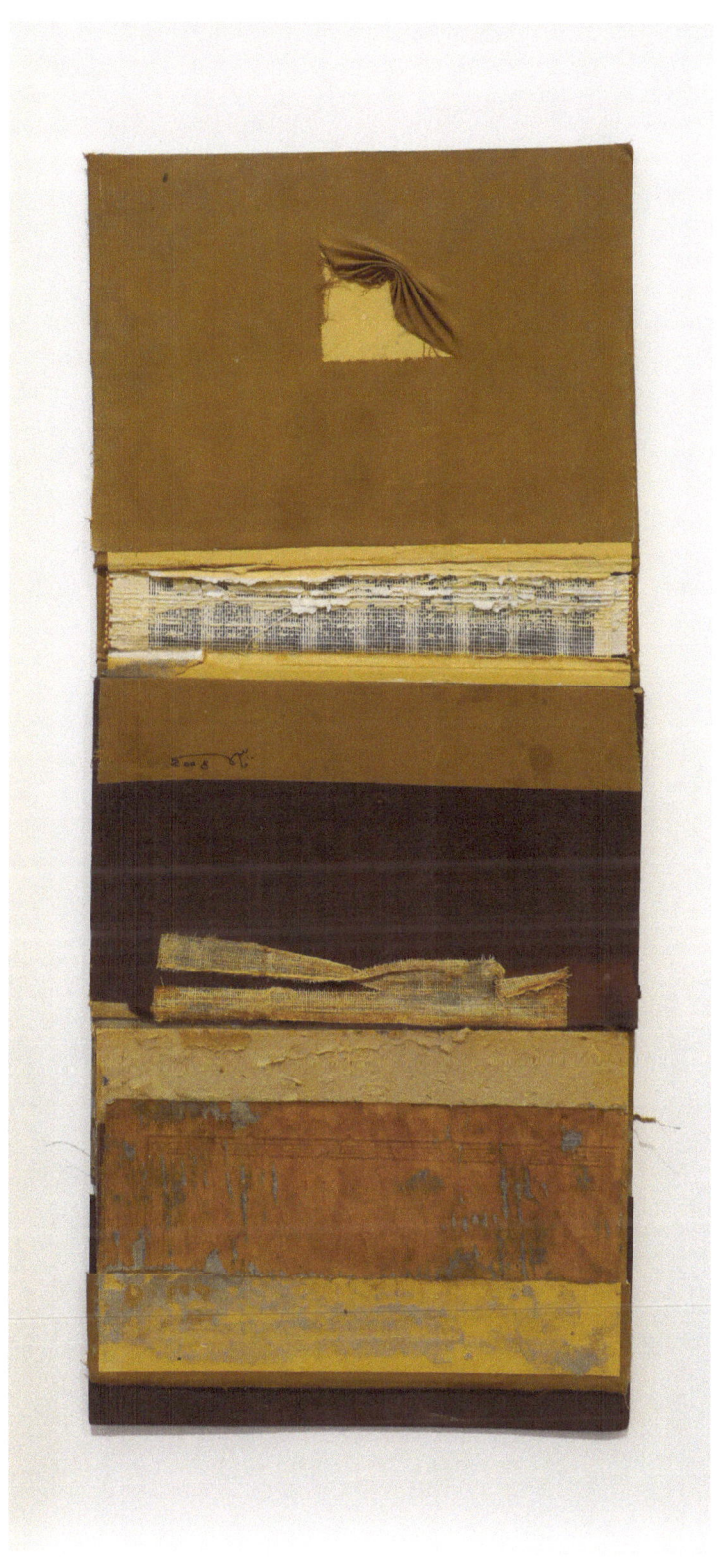

ARTISTS' STATEMENTS

HAYDER ALI

The continuing wars and terrorism have left deep and painful scars in the memory of the Iraqi people. These wars have not been neat and clean, or fresh and dry, without consequences. There is not a body or soul left untouched in Iraq. The wars made deep wounds that have become part of our soul, so they can never be forgotten.

My art books, or *Dafatir*, are part of my mourning for the National Library of Iraq, which was assassinated by the hands of the new Mongols, uncontrollable mobs and terrorists. My books are witnesses to a period of catastrophe that has driven nails into the body of our culture and our civilization's achievements.

My works are also about reprocessing the elements of our environment. Throughout our long history, Mesopotamian culture is full of such examples. I took elements such as the book and the palm frond and altered their usual use, releasing their buried and inherent expressive power and re-presenting them as art.

My oil paintings are also part of this vast memory of human interaction with the environment. They are loaded with such memory—conscious and unconscious. The result is a true expression of the harmony of nature and the human condition, symbolizing the concerns of humanity and the community. They remind us that beauty is not just memory past but a work in progress.

Time and movement are two connected concepts in my works. Movement has a circular shape, a life cycle that transfers from beginning until the end. In a single moment or a whole lifetime, the present is constantly moving to the past, and vice versa. Time practices its existence without the need of the mechanical controls and calculations of an alarm clock. Art is an internal meditation concerned with understanding and expressing the external world.

From "Contemporary Iraqi Art," Pomegranate Gallery, 2007

AMAL ALWAN

In 1975, when I was in primary school, Al Doroobi, who is now one of the oldest artists in Iraq, saw my drawings and agreed to teach me. He became my teacher and mentor. He gave me oil paints and other supplies, and he encouraged me. This is how I began as an artist and painter.

While studying at the university, I exhibited in many galleries. Since 1982, I have exhibited in private galleries with other artists in Baghdad. I married in 1991, the year that the U.S. sanctions took effect, and I stopped painting because we did not have much money.

In 1995, I was working as a teacher, earning only $1.50 an hour under the sanctions regime, when I met Voices in the Wilderness, a group formed to challenge the economic warfare being waged by the U.S. against the people of Iraq. The members of Voices encouraged me to resume painting and helped me to sell in the U.S.

Three days before the U.S. military occupation of Iraq, we left for Syria.

When we returned to Al Karada our house had been looted. We began working to furnish it, but two months later it was destroyed by U.S. bombing. In 2004, we decided to leave Iraq. We went to Amman and applied for permission to enter the U.S. It was not granted, so we stayed in Amman. We enrolled our children in school, and I resumed my studies in economics and continued painting.

When we left Amman to renew our three month statutes, the border of Jordan refused to allow us to reenter Amman. Today, we are stuck in Baghdad. Our children were not able to resume their schooling in Amman. We live without a house or income. I work with humanity.org and as an independent journalist. Both positions are unpaid.

My friends are my support system, helping me to market and sell my work, which is my family's only income. My husband has yet to find work after returning from 12 years in the Iraqi Army. We have three children—Abeer, 15, Omar, 11, and Ali, 7.

From "Contemporary Iraqi Art," Pomegranate Gallery, 2007

ODED HALAHMY

The Hebrew letters found in my artwork are inspired by a Hebrew children's song in Iraq, called the "Alef Bet" song. My favorite part of the song was singing "hey wow," letters that were easy to say and opened the mouth. I loved singing those two letters. Western Jews pronounce the letter as "vav," but Babylonian Jews pronounced it "wow."

Hey is the 5th letter in the Hebrew alphabet, which represents many things: it is the first letter of the name of god. The word *chamsa* refers to the five digits on the hand, and is derived from the root word for the number five in Hebrew. *Khamsa* is also the Arabic word for five. The imagery and symbolism of the open hand has long been a popular amulet for magical protection from the evil eye, like a stop sign. I incorporate the image of the chamsa artistically in many different forms and shapes in my sculptures and Chanukah lamps.

Wow, the sixth letter, opens the mouth as it is spoken, relating it to the sense of sound. It can also symbolize the six-pointed Star of David, and also is a symbol of harmony of the male and female. It represents love, balance, and help to other beings. It is the letter of life, and as a letter it is the link between all parts.

Together, these letters have become part of my Pomegranate Alphabet.

I love pomegranates. They are the jewels of the autumn; in my opinion there is nothing in the world more sensual. The exterior of the pomegranate is seductive and tempting, and its round body is full of seeds. Round and full, pomegranates are an ancient and universal symbol of beauty, love and marriage, fertility, prosperity, hope, life, and rebirth. It is said that if you dream of pomegranates, you will be as blessed as the pomegranate is full of seeds. I cannot eat one in a hurry or as quickly as I can any other fruit. You must have lots of patience with them, and you must be gentle opening them. Upon opening a pomegranate, I can see beautiful secrets within. Beneath the fruit's skin you will find

ODED HALAHMY (continued)

juicy seeds, jewel-like, each carefully packed in a separate compartment. I am relaxed when I am eating a pomegranate. It is only then that I feel that I have all the time in the world. I give to you a pomegranate with love and hopes for a generous future.

I sculpt with the idea of harmony in my heart, from the beauty of Jerusalem, Babylon, and New York. I use the ancient languages of my mother and father's tongue in my art: Biblical Hebrew, Arabic, English, and so on. In particular, the book of Song of Songs of King Solomon in the Bible has been a source of inspiration for my art, as my father and mother knew it by heart and would recite it frequently. My identity in my artwork reflects both Middle Eastern elements and Western.

The beauty in my artwork is that it is not political, allowing me unrestricted freedom to create, wherever I am in the world. I have always created art from nothing, from objects and wood scraps I find on the street. Even the texture found on my artwork is from the sawdust created from the cutting of the wood shapes. When I clean and sweep my studio, I carefully sort and collect the sawdust (what comes to mind is how my father used to collect the gold shavings from sweeping his goldsmith machine shop in Baghdad). I mix the sawdust with glue and paint a landscape of texture onto the surface of my art. When I am making a new artwork, I feel connected to a higher power and I feel we are in harmony. My home is my temple; it is within me. The sun always shines and my cup is always full.

I wish that all nations would live in harmony. I have a special wish that the children of Abraham will live in peace with each other.

MOHAMMED AL HAMADANY

LAYLAT AN NAR (NIGHT OF FIRE)
This unprecedented series of paintings depicts an Iraqi perspective of 'Shock and Awe', the 2003 campaign to oust Saddam Hussein. Mohmammed al Hamadany truly welcomed Americans as liberators who freed Iraq from his brother's murderer, but the rampant chaos of the campaign cast an eerie glare of ambivalence over his canvas. In its truest form, "Night of Fire" reveals the messy interconnectedness of violence, the profane reality of collateral damage. The central piece of the "Night of Fire" depicts the fall of Saddam Hussein's statue in Firdos Square. Ironically, Mohammed depicts the cheering onlookers as monkey-like because, "the same people also clapped when the statue went up."

THE MURDER OF MOHAMMED'S BROTHER
Mohammed al Hamadany is the brother of Iraq's former Minister of Planning, a man lauded internationally as the brains behind Iraq, and then murdered by Saddam Hussein in 1979. The murder was purely political—a successful effort by Saddam Hussein to consolidate power upon seizing the presidency and thereby preventing the merger of Iraq and Syria. The following excerpt from *The Atlantic Monthly* (May, 2002) by Mark Bowden describes the event:

"On July 18, 1979, [Saddam] invited all the members of the Revolutionary Command Council and hundreds of other party leaders to a conference hall in Baghdad. He had a video camera running in the back of the hall to record the event for posterity. Wearing his military uniform, he walked slowly to the lectern and stood behind two microphones, gesturing with a big cigar. His body and broad face seemed weighted down with sadness. There had been a betrayal, he said. A Syrian plot. There were traitors among them. Then Saddam took a seat, and Muhyi Abd al-Hussein Mashhadi, the secretary-general of the Command Council, appeared from behind a curtain to confess his own involvement in the putsch.

From "Oil on Landscape," Pomegranate Gallery, 2009

MOHAMMED AL HAMADANY (continued)

He had been secretly arrested and tortured days before; now he spilled out dates, times, and places where the plotters had met. Then he started naming names. As he fingered members of the audience one by one, armed guards grabbed the accused and escorted them from the hall. When one man shouted that he was innocent, Saddam shouted back, "Itla! Itla!"—"Get out! Get out!" (Weeks later, after secret trials, Saddam had the mouths of the accused taped shut so that they could utter no troublesome last words before their firing squads.) When all of the sixty "traitors" had been removed, Saddam again took the podium and wiped tears from his eyes as he repeated the names of those who had betrayed him. Some in the audience, too, were crying—perhaps out of fear. This chilling performance had the desired effect. Everyone in the hall now understood exactly how things would work in Iraq from that day forward. The audience rose and began clapping, first in small groups and finally as one. The session ended with cheers and laughter. The remaining "leaders"—about 300 in all—left the hall shaken, grateful to have avoided the fate of their colleagues, and certain that one man now controlled the destiny of their entire nation. Videotapes of the purge were circulated throughout the country."

ISMAIL KHAYAT

With the "Anfal Memory" series, Ismail Khayat, the former head of Kurdistan's Art Department of the Ministry of Culture, honors the 182,000 Kurds who were killed by order of Saddam Hussein. Painted in watercolor and India ink, the masks are boldly expressive and colorful, yet stand as memorials created by an artist who escaped the terrible genocide.

Khayat was born in Khanaken, Kurdistan in 1944, and has been a member of the Iraqi Artist Association since 1965 and the Iraqi Artist Syndicate since 1970. After teaching art in Sulaymania for twenty-four years, he became supervisor of all arts activities in the region, curating numerous art exhibitions throughout Iraq and participating in sixty-five group exhibitions and international exhibitions in Damascus, Jordan, Paris, Japan, Sweden, Russia, Eastern Europe, and South Korea.

His work can be found in many European and Japanese private collections, and twenty-five of his works are owned by the Iraqi National Museum. Khayat's prior visit to the United States was in the summer of 2001, when he participated in the special seminar, "Civil Life in Iraqi Kurdistan" in Washington, DC.

From "Contemporary Iraqi Art," Pomegranate Gallery, 2007

HANAA MALALLAH

Hanaa Malallah is a painter and printmaker in Baghdad. She is widely regarded as the leading female artist from Iraq. Hanaa received her B.F.A., M.F.A., and doctoral degree in the philosophy of art from the Academy of Fine Arts in Baghdad. She continues to teach and lecture at the college while pursuing her painting. She points to Shakir Hassan Al Sayad, one of the Iraqi "Pioneers" of the 1950s, as her most influential teacher.

"I loved and respected him not only because he taught me how to paint, but because he taught me how to write, how to live, and how to incorporate mysticism in my life and my art."

Notable among Hanaa's exhibitions are the National Museum of Modern Art in Amman, Jordan (1997); the Institute du Monde Arabe in Paris (2000); and "Women Artists of the Islamic World" sponsored by UNESCO in Spain and Paris (2003).

Her works have been exhibited in London galleries, first with the "Strokes of Genius" exhibition at Brunei Gallery (2000) and at the "Expressions of Hope" exhibition at Ayagallery (2003). Her works are held by the Royal Jordanian Museum and private collections worldwide.

Says Malallah: I approach the abstract plane through a "pile of forms," shape, text, numbers and colors. A density is reached beyond figurative clarity, which is black with accumulation. My works, when made of wood, are uncoated, naked; when of paper, open to creasing and folding. I approach making art not by dominating, but rather by following and reacting with the material's character. My works appear as "ruins," the cycle of destruction visited upon my city, Baghdad: its desecration and humiliation, I'm economic with color. In nature a leaf may be green for whatever reason, but in painting, why?

From "Contemporary Iraqi Art," Pomegranate Gallery, 2007

HASSAN MASSOUDY

Hassan Massoudy was born in Iraq in 1944, and at the age of seventeen, he began working with calligraphers in Baghdad for the next eight years. In June 1969, he attended The School of Fine Arts in Paris, France, and has lived there ever since.

Massoudy's creations came out from the meeting of the past and present, Eastern art and Western art, and tradition and modernity. He has perpetuated the tradition of calligraphy as craft while also breaking tradition at the same time. Massoudy simplifies lines, tending to purer lines and adding color. In his work, Massoudy introduces signs, letters, words and sentences, at times borrowing phrases from famous poets and great writers.

Massoudy explains how poetry becomes calligraphy: "I count the straight letters then the curves so as to be able to create a rhythm by composing them. I dream about those letters. I imagine the word in different styles of calligraphy. I sketch a few lines, transforming the letters, I move them around, adjust them.

The line, as a dynamic force, and in its adequate relation with the meaning of words, must reflect two things: on the one hand strength and rigor, on the other abandon and grace. The line's aspect must suggest a direction: a pushing or pulling gesture, quick or slow, heavy or light, calm or bursting forth.

Calligraphy is like all the other arts, the expression of happiness and suffering go side by side. Do and undo, and grow through each experience."

From "Contemporary Iraqi Art," Pomegranate Gallery, 2007

NAZIHA RASHID

Naziha Rashid was born in 1932 in Baghdad, where she received her Bachelor's degree in Arabic language and literature. She earned a diploma in drawing and painting at The Institute of Fine Arts in Baghdad, a National Diploma in Design scholarship in painting at Chelsea School of Art in London, and a Master's Degree in creative arts from the University of Maryland. Naziha has worked as a college professor and as a consultant for exhibitions sponsored by Islamic Educational Scientific and Cultural Organization (ISESCO), office of the Arab League, Rabat, Morocco. She has lived in New York since 1994, and has retired and devoted herself to her passion, which is art.

"I try to keep my work simple and clear yet elegant, while maintaining a core of spirituality from Iraq, birthplace of prophets and the greatest of civilizations, and from Baghdad, birthplace of wonders, magic and imagination."

"I feel a great nostalgia for my dear country...which has been ravaged by wars and is still caught in the grip of struggle and destruction. I seek refuge in painting villages and the countryside, which are steeped in folklore, beautiful old traditions, and a kind of security so different from the current state of affairs. It is a vision of hope... My colors include earthy tones like ochre, red, burnt amber, and brown. I also use the colors of the dawn and the heat of the sun."

"The village woman is the central figure in my paintings, and everything else...supports her presence. She is not just an afterthought or an ornament but rather of central importance in life. Beauty graces her seated figure or while at work. I depict her in different aspects, both happy and sad, and as a mother. Folkloric symbols are prevalent in my paintings: a full moon, a crescent moon, a hand, a bird, tribal tattoos..."

"...I strive in my work to create a world that is beautiful and full of love, hope, and optimism that revolves around happiness and security no matter how difficult or ugly conditions become around the world."

From "Contemporary Iraqi Art," Pomegranate Gallery, 2007

QASIM SABTI

Born in Baghdad in 1953, Qasim Sabti became crippled as a seven-month-old baby. Since he grew up in a neighborhood with many athletes who were local heroes, he won attention by distinguishing himself with his artistic abilities. As a teenager, students would pay him a falafel sandwich for a drawing, or for one of his poems or love letters in beautiful Arabic calligraphy.

Upon graduating from the Academy of Fine Arts in Baghdad in 1980, Sabti established a workshop for Arabic calligraphy and painting. Beginning in 1985, he taught at the Baghdad University of Technology, and in 1986 participated in the first Baghdad International Biennial. In 1987, he returned to the Academy of Fine Arts to teach painting.

In 1992, Sabti founded the Hewar Art Gallery in Baghdad, which has since become an important and active oasis for Iraqi artists (*Hewar* means dialogue).

Steve Mumford, a New York-based artist who was embedded with the coalition troops during several extended stays, described Sabti as "a charismatic, handsome man in his 50s, who holds court most mornings in the gallery and the garden in the back, where there is a charming café, surrounded by lush plants and sheltered from the sun by a corrugated tin roof supported by antique columns. It's the greenest place I've seen in Iraq, and on this particular October morning it's buzzing with energy, with groups of men and a few women talking animatedly." Mumford, who has received critical recognition for his watercolors documenting scenes in Baghdad, said that "Artists of Qasim's generation were the students of the 'Pioneers,' the first generation of Iraqi artists to bring modernism to Iraq."

Currently, Sabti serves as Vice-President of Iraqi Plastic Artists Society, which has 1,780 members. He is also Secretary of the Iraqi Cultural Council. His paintings are in private collections throughout Europe, the Middle East, the United States, Japan, and Korea.

From "Contemporary Iraqi Art," Pomegranate Gallery, 2007

QASIM SABTI (continued)

A TALE OF THE PHOENIX

In April, 2003, the bombings took a heavy toll on Baghdad. Many parts of the city were reduced to rubble. Worse, chaos broke out in the streets, driving the city into utter hell.

The morning after that first sleepless night I went to check on a place most dear to me, the Academy of Fine Arts. It was here that I had studied and enhanced my artistic skills. To my dismay, the Academy's street was littered with books, and pages torn from them blew in the dry wind. As I entered the Academy's library, my senses were abruptly confronted by an acrid smoke that silently drifted above irregular mounds of charred books. In that instant discovery combined with pain, I saw that my beloved Academy had become another victim of a mob out of control. They had emptied the library shelves and set the books afire. The destruction was total. As I walked about, the pressure of my feet on damp and partially burned pages seemed to gently squeeze more pungent odors into the silence around me. I realized that a new bitterness in the air was the source of my tears. I just couldn't be certain how much of those tears were caused by the smoke and how much were from being emotionally distraught.

I felt like a fireman desperately in need of finding survivors. As I pushed through the piles, I noticed a few books that, although covered with soot, appeared to have survived. That's when I spotted a book with a pale yellow cover. As I picked it up, I felt my fingers shaking. I brushed off the soot. Here was a survey of beautiful Russian landscape paintings. Suddenly, just as I started to turn the pages, the book collapsed. The whole block of pages, first weakened by the fire and later by the water, dropped from its spine. The pages scattered around me on the damp dirty floor.

Now I held only the cloth cover. Looking closer, I was haunted by the little details of life that filled the inside cover: strips of cotton, some Arabic verses scribbled in pencil, notes written by the librarian. My

From "Contemporary Iraqi Art," Pomegranate Gallery, 2007

imagination was reborn. Here I found the essence of life deeply inscribed as signs of one book's extensive journey. I was filled with a new sense of life and hope. I also found it visually inspiring. Like the fireman realizing that some victims were still breathing, I began to gather together more covers that called to me. The appearance of the cover was most important. Collectively, these books challenged me to bring them back to life from their graveyard floor.

I brought a pile of the damaged covers back to my studio and immediately started to work. With passionate fingers, I started to transform them. First, I rubbed their surfaces to remove much of their previous literary appearance. Next, I cut swatches from the covers, punched holes, re-applied loose delicate strings and lacey webbings, and even painted on them. In the process, I was ever-mindful that these books once documented so many great achievements in world history. Once, they had been valuable resources for the people of Iraq. Now, in their transformed state, these collages were bringing back life to books whose texts had been completely destroyed. These works of art are newly-derived from sacred bones. As such, they should stand as symbolic documents of the resilience of cultural life. They are also my attempt to gain victory over the destruction surrounding us in Baghdad.

EXHIBITION
CHECKLIST

HAYDER ALI

Untitled, 2004
Oil on wood
24 x 24 in.

Black Talk, 2005
Mixed media on paper
9¼ x 13¼ in.

America, 2005
Mixed media on paper
9¼ x 13¼ in.

Memory Wall, 2006
Mixed media on paper
10¼ x 14 in.

Elite, 2007
Mixed media on cardboard
10¼ x 14 in.

AMAL ALWAN

Basrah, n.d.
Oil on canvas
25 x 17 in.

Blue Domed Mosque, n.d.
Oil on canvas
25½ x 17½ in.

ODED HALAHMY

Walking Home, 2004
Cast bronze
40½ x 29 x 11¾ in.

Five Six Singing (Study), 2013
Cast bronze
20 x 6¾ x 6 in.

Sing Hey Wow, 2013
Cast bronze, No. 208 (ED5)
32½ x 13¾ x 8½ in.

Reading Hey Wow, 2013
Cast bronze
20 x 6¾ x 6 in.

MOHAMMED AL HAMADANY

Untitled, from the series "Night of Fire (Laylat an Nar)," n.d.
Oil and acrylic on canvas
68 x 12½ in.

Untitled, from the series "Night of Fire (Laylat an Nar)," n.d.
Oil and acrylic on canvas
68 x 12½ in.

ISMAIL KHAYAT

Untitled, from the series
"Anfal Memory," 2006
Ink and pigment on watercolor paper
11½ x 7½ in.

Untitled, from the series
"Anfal Memory," 2006
Ink and pigment on watercolor paper
11½ x 7½ in.

Untitled, from the series
"Anfal Memory," 2006
Ink and pigment on watercolor paper
11½ x 7½ in.

Untitled, from the series
"Anfal Memory," 2006
Ink and pigment on watercolor paper
11½ x 7½ in.

Untitled, from the series
"Anfal Memory," 2006
Ink and pigment on watercolor paper
11½ x 7½ in.

Untitled, from the series
"Anfal Memory," 2006
Ink and pigment on watercolor paper
11½ x 7½ in.

HANAA MALALLAH

Uruk Old Love, 2006
Mixed media on carved wood
15½ x 15½ in.

Uruk Wall, 2006
Mixed media on carved wood
15½ x 15½ in.

HASSAN MASSOUDY

Sur terre, il y a place pour
tous, Schiller, 2006
Water–based pigments on paper
29½ x 21¾ in.

The love that I hold for you, that is
my eternal delight / The passion
that I swear to you, this is my religion,
Ibn Zaydoun 11th century, 2008
Water–based pigments on paper
29 x 23 in.

NAZIHA RASHID

Woman in the Village, 1999
Watercolor and gouache on paper
14 x 11 in.

Nostalgic, 2000
Acrylic on canvas
19 x 16 in.

Evil Eye, 2003
Watercolor, gouache,
and ink on paper
8½ x 11 in.

In the Market, 2006
Watercolor and acrylic on paper
13 x 19 in.

QASIM SABTI

Untitled, from the series "Book
Cover Collage," n.d.
Book cover and collage
15¼ x 9½ in.

Untitled, from the series "Book
Cover Collage," 2006
Book cover and collage
12½ x 8½ in.

Untitled, from the series "Book
Cover Collage," 2006
Book cover and collage
14⅞ x 8¾ in.

Untitled, from the series "Book
Cover Collage," 2008
Book cover and collage
18¾ x 8¼ in.

www.ingramcontent.com/pod-product-compliance
Lightning Source LLC
Chambersburg PA
CBHW050851180526
45159CB00007B/2645